POTES SUITE FOR FLUTE AND GUITAR

by LARRY HAMMETT and MIRANDA ARANA - *NUCLEAR OKRA*

To access the online audio go to: **www.melbay.com/30885MEB**

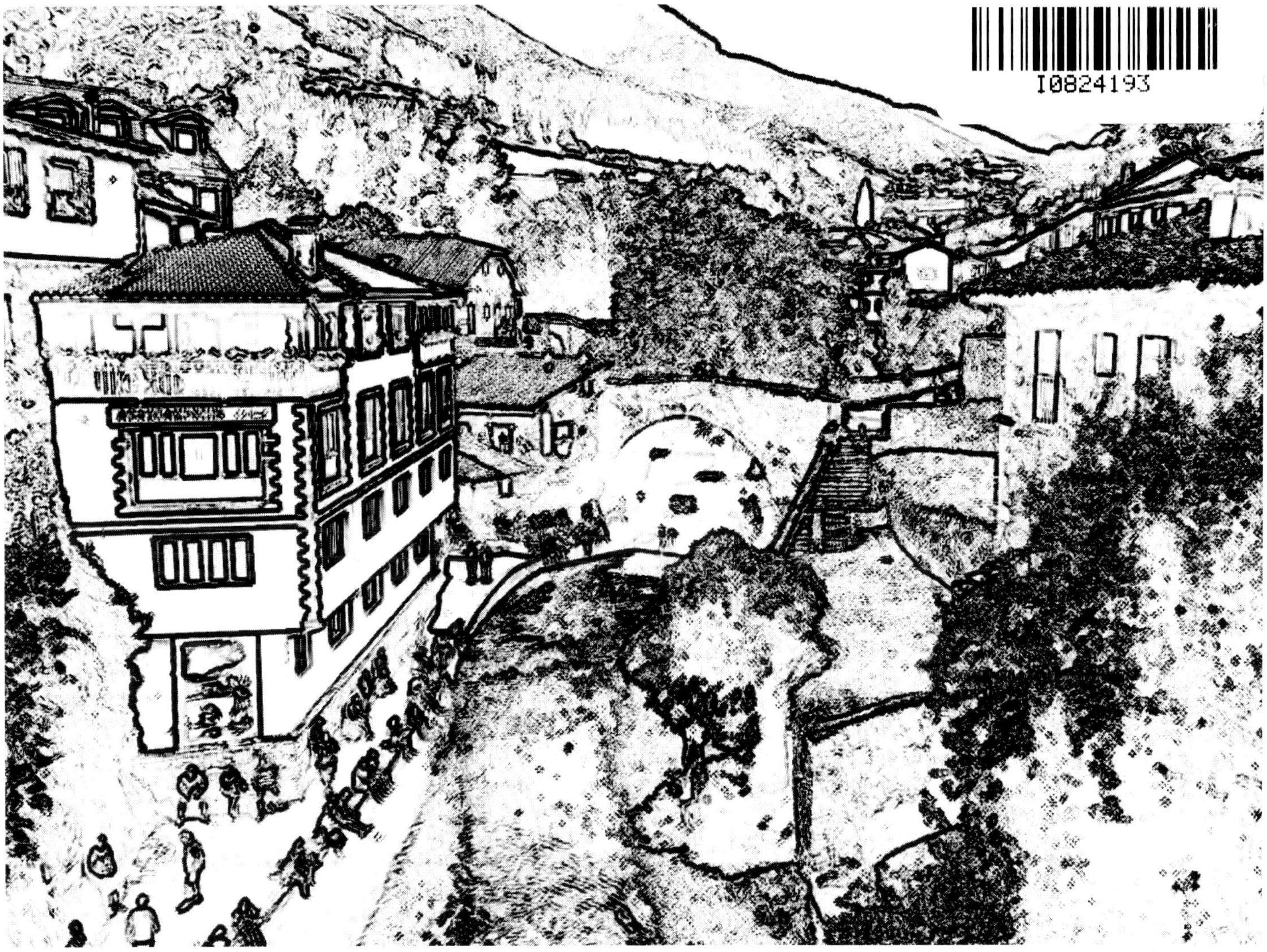

Watercolor painting used on front cover is courtesy of the artist, Angeliki Stringou.

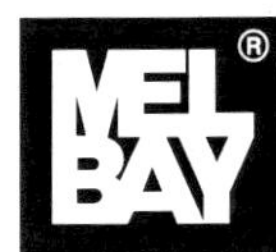

WWW.MELBAY.COM

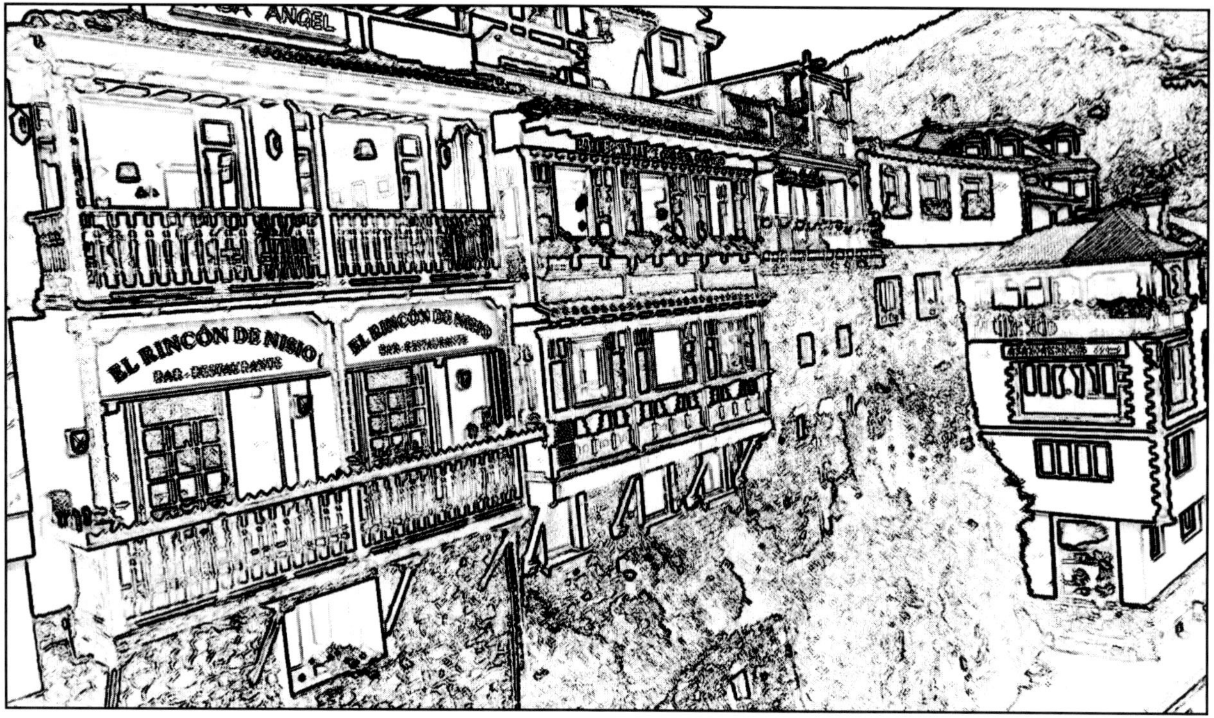

Note to Musicians:

Performers are encouraged to take liberties with articulation, dynamics, tempo, and embellishments. Videos and audio recordings of these pieces are available on YouTube, and also upon request. We can be reached at nuclearokra@gmail.com, or via our Facebook page at www.facebook.com/nuclearokra. We hope you enjoy the adventure of learning and playing these pieces!

Miranda Arana & Larry Hammett December 2020

About the Potes Suite:

In the summer of 2018, while traveling in Northern Spain, we fell in love with the medieval town of Potes (pictured above) and the mountains, culture and people of Liébana in western Cantabria. We stayed in Potes for three weeks, during which time we made friends, explored the town, and hiked the extensive trails in the surrounding area. Inspired by our experiences, we composed this suite of four movements for flute and guitar. The *Potes Suite* attempts to convey Potes as a place of great beauty and magic. We have performed the *Potes Suite* in Armenia, Turkey, Spain, France, Greece, Bosnia-Herzegovina, and the United States.

About the Composers:

Miranda Arana and Larry Hammett teach music courses at the University of Oklahoma's School of Music. Larry has been the coordinator of the guitar program since 1991, teaching classical and jazz guitar. As a flutist, Miranda has played classical, Latin American, Vietnamese, Middle Eastern, and Irish music. They have performed together as colleagues in various music ensembles since 2001. In 2017 they began performing as the duo Nuclear Okra. Inspired by travel around the world, their compositions are an exciting blend of stylistic elements and techniques.

Potes Suite

For Flute and Guitar

1. La Viorna **Score:** pages 4 - 8 / **Flute:** pages 4 - 5 / **Guitar:** pages 3 - 7

Overlooking the village of Potes is a majestic mountain called La Viorna that lies at the edge of the eastern massif of the Picos de Europa. At the peak sits a huge white cross that stands guard to a monastery perched midway below. While it is sometimes shrouded in clouds, on clear days, we could see the cross from the terrace of our apartment and from other vantage points along the hiking trails that weave up and down the adjacent mountains. This piece is a sonic illustration of our journey up to the summit of La Viorna, with its changing landscapes, a gentle rain, the sound of bells from grazing sheep, the cross, the beautiful vistas, and the soaring birds.

2. Rio Quiviesa **Score:** pages 10 -13 / **Flute:** pages 6-7 / **Guitar:** pages 8-11

Two rivers run through the middle of the town of Potes; the Deva and its tributary, the Quiviesa. Through the village, the rivers are lined with stone footpaths that weave under ancient stone bridges. Beyond the village, the rivers weave through forests and fields, often hidden from view under dense foliage. We bought inner tubes from a local auto shop, hiked a few kilometers out of town, got in the river, and rode the inner tubes back to town. This piece attempts to capture the excitement of maneuvering through unknown twisting, narrow, rocky channels and rushing water. Upon reaching town after a forty-minute run, we returned back to our starting point and took the journey a second time!

3. Monasterio de Santo Toribio **Score:** pp. 15 - 23 / **Flute:** 8-11 / **Guitar:** 12-17

The Monastery of Santo Toribio of Liébana lies just 3 kilometers west of Potes, near the base of La Viorna. It is an important holy site for Roman Catholics and a popular tourist destination. Thousands of visitors make pilgrimages every year to view and kiss a fragment of wood that is believed to be the biggest surviving piece of the original cross upon which Jesus Christ was crucified. We composed this piece to commemorate our own adventure there, and to celebrate the yearning for spiritual nourishment that motivates human beings to embark on pilgrimages all over the world. We use a Tibetan prayer bowl at the beginning of the piece to establish the idea of a sacred atmosphere. The original composition employed a dual-chambered wooden ocarina for a small portion of the piece, to represent the sound of a conch shell or horn signaling a call to prayer, but this part has been scored for silver flute for practical reasons.

4. Retratos de Potes **Score:** pp. 25 - 31 / **Flute:** 12-14 / **Guitar:** 18-24

The village of Potes sits at the confluence of four valleys. The town itself is a maze of rock pathways, stone stairways, bustling shops and restaurants, houses, balconies, and rivers running under ancient bridges. The town retains its medieval atmosphere despite the bustle of modern life, the influx of tourism, and the surprising number of immigrants from all over the world who have chosen to live in Potes. This piece is our musical attempt to reflect the many layers of history and humanity of this beautiful town.

La Viorna

Hammett/Arana

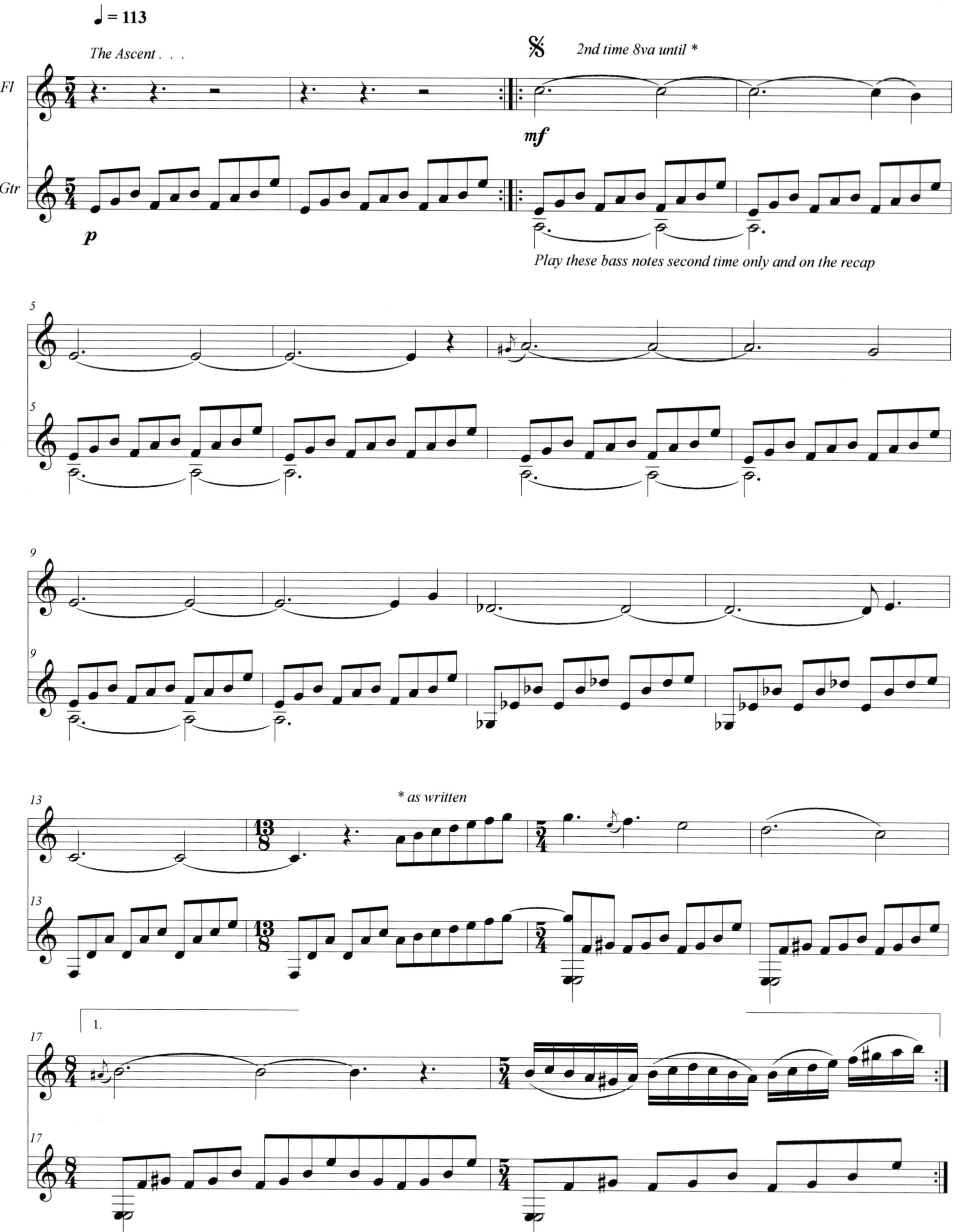

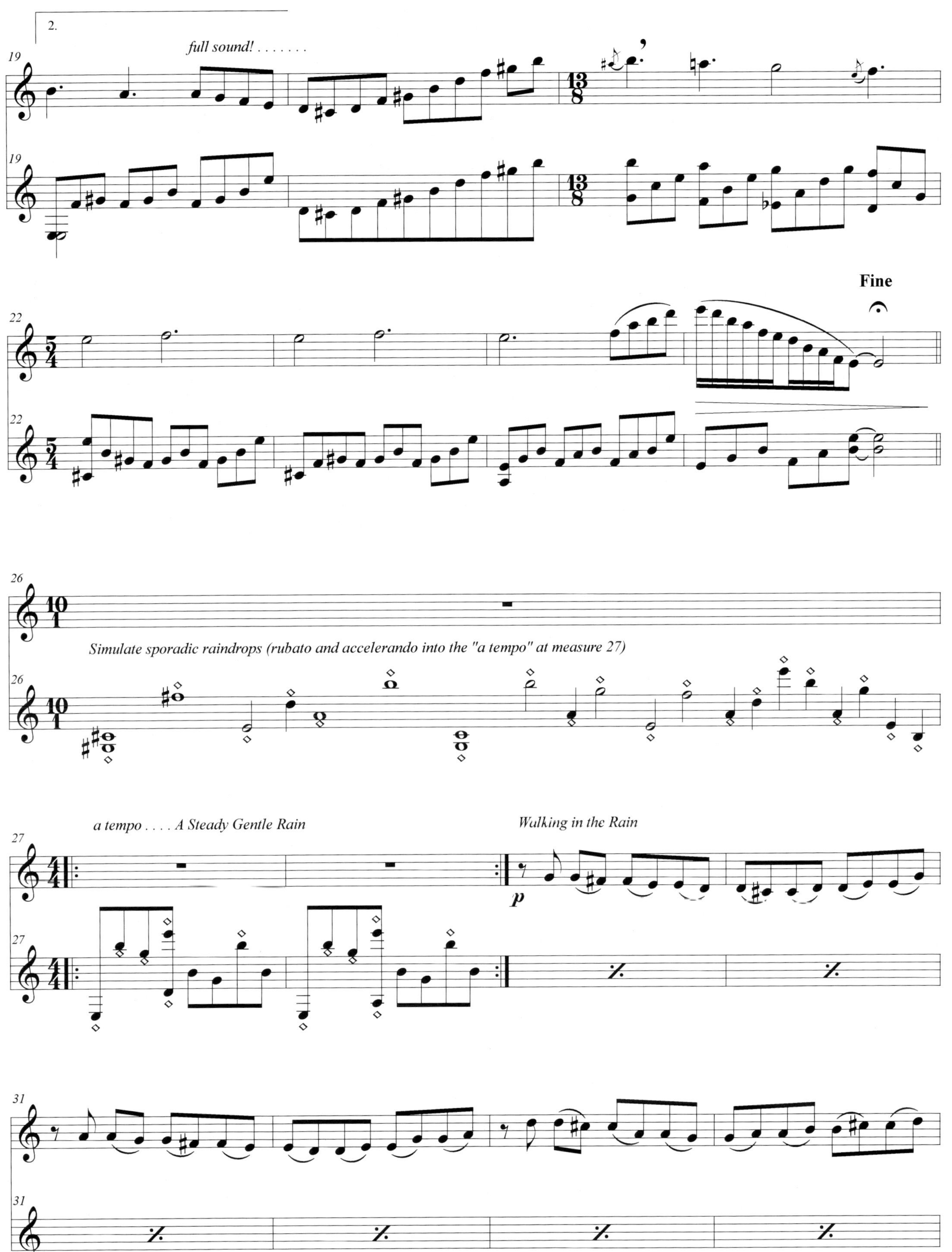

2.
full sound! . . . .
Fine
Simulate sporadic raindrops (rubato and accelerando into the "a tempo" at measure 27)
a tempo . . . . A Steady Gentle Rain
Walking in the Rain
p

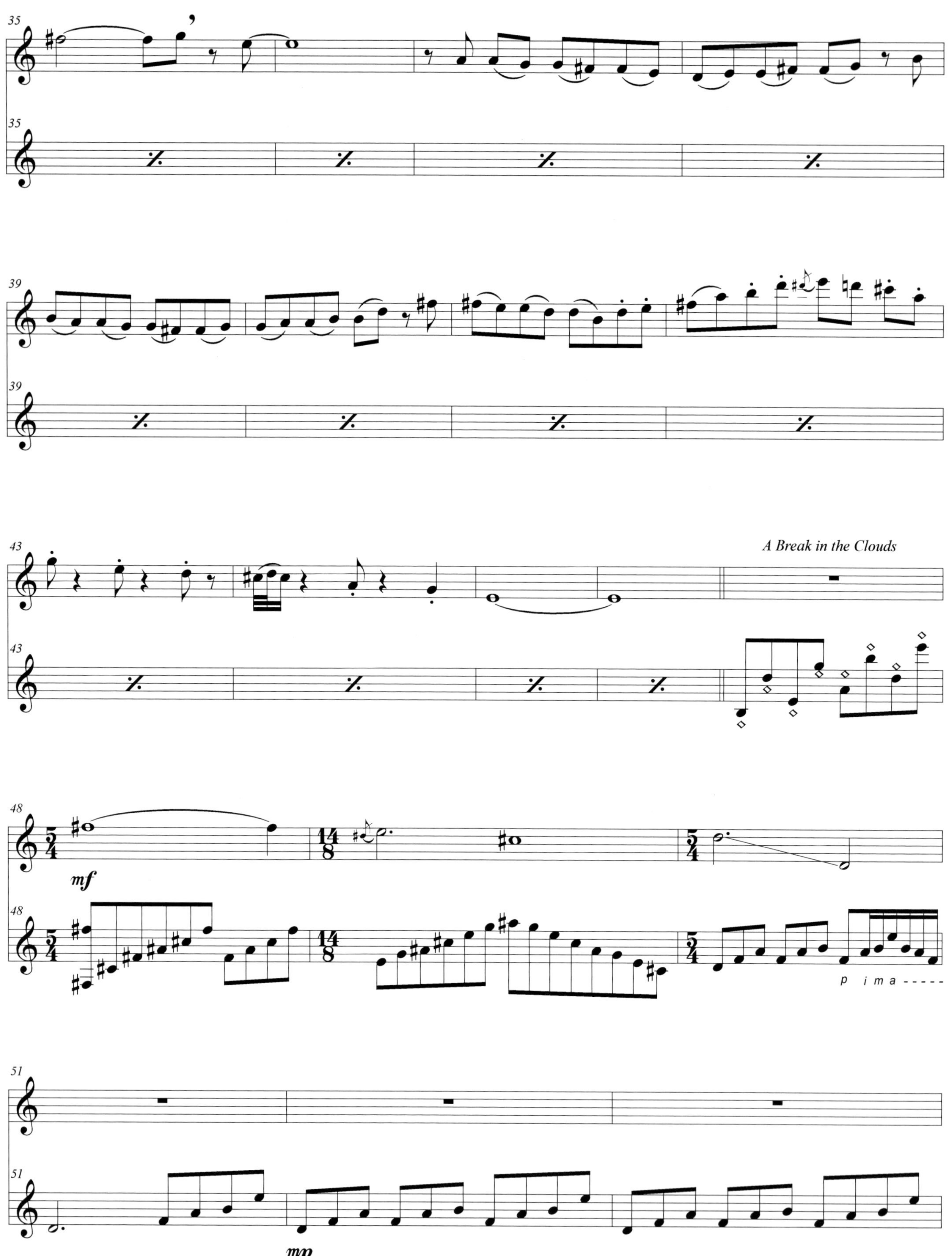
35
35
39
39
43
A Break in the Clouds
43
48
mf
48
p i m a
51
51
mp

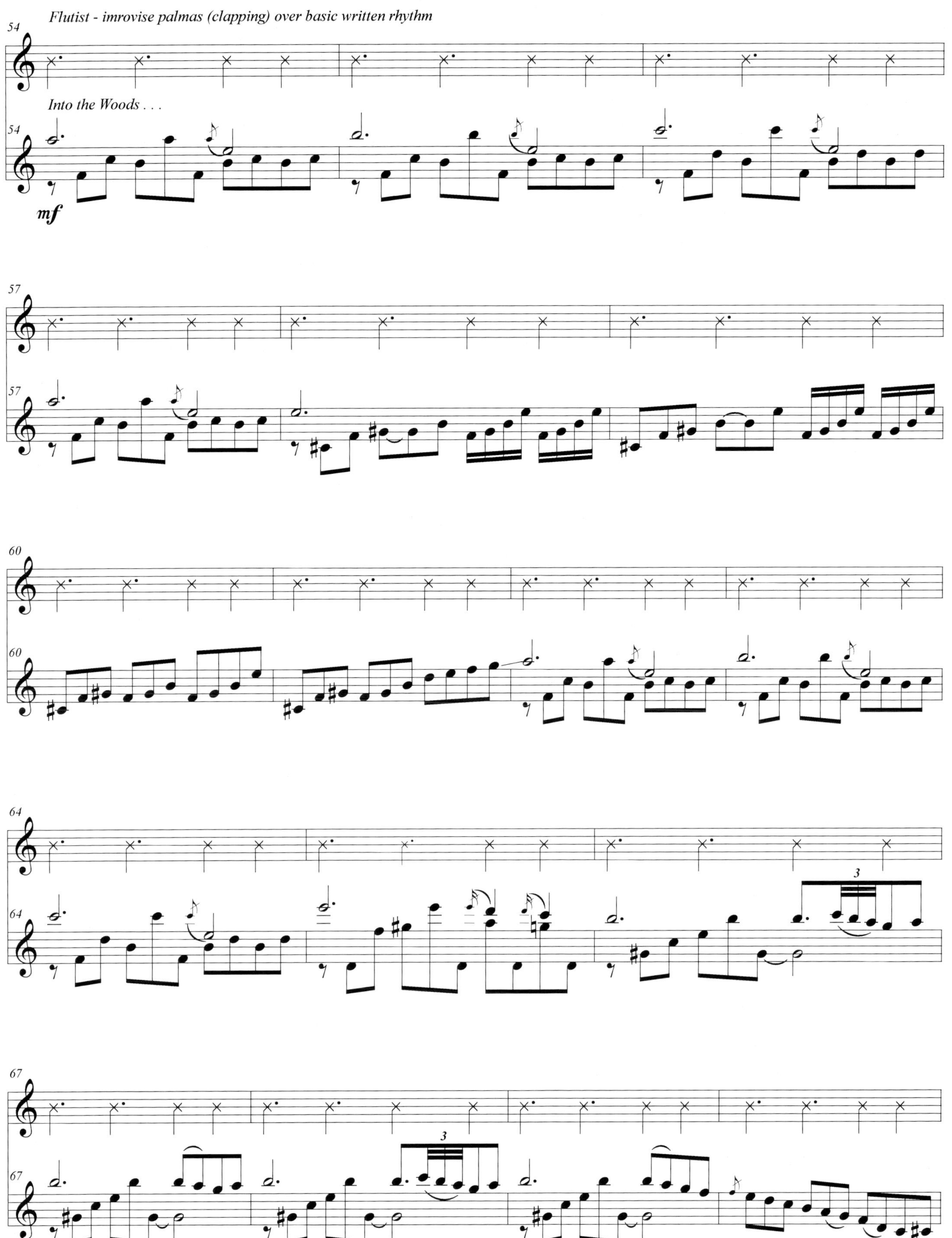
Flutist - imrovise palmas (clapping) over basic written rhythm
Into the Woods . . .
mf

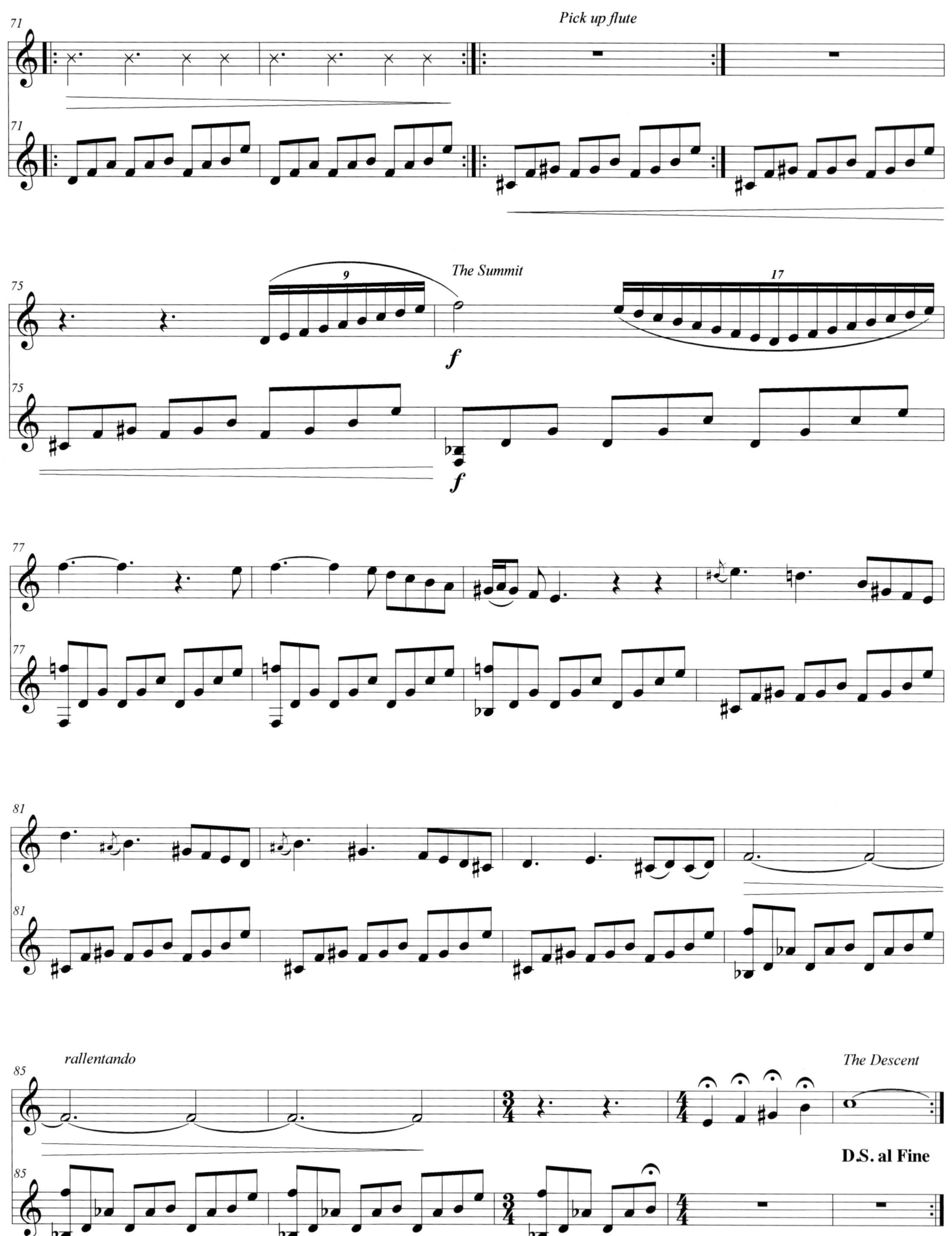

71
Pick up flute
75
9
The Summit
17
f
77
81
85
rallentando
3
4
The Descent
D.S. al Fine

La Viorna, Potes, Spain

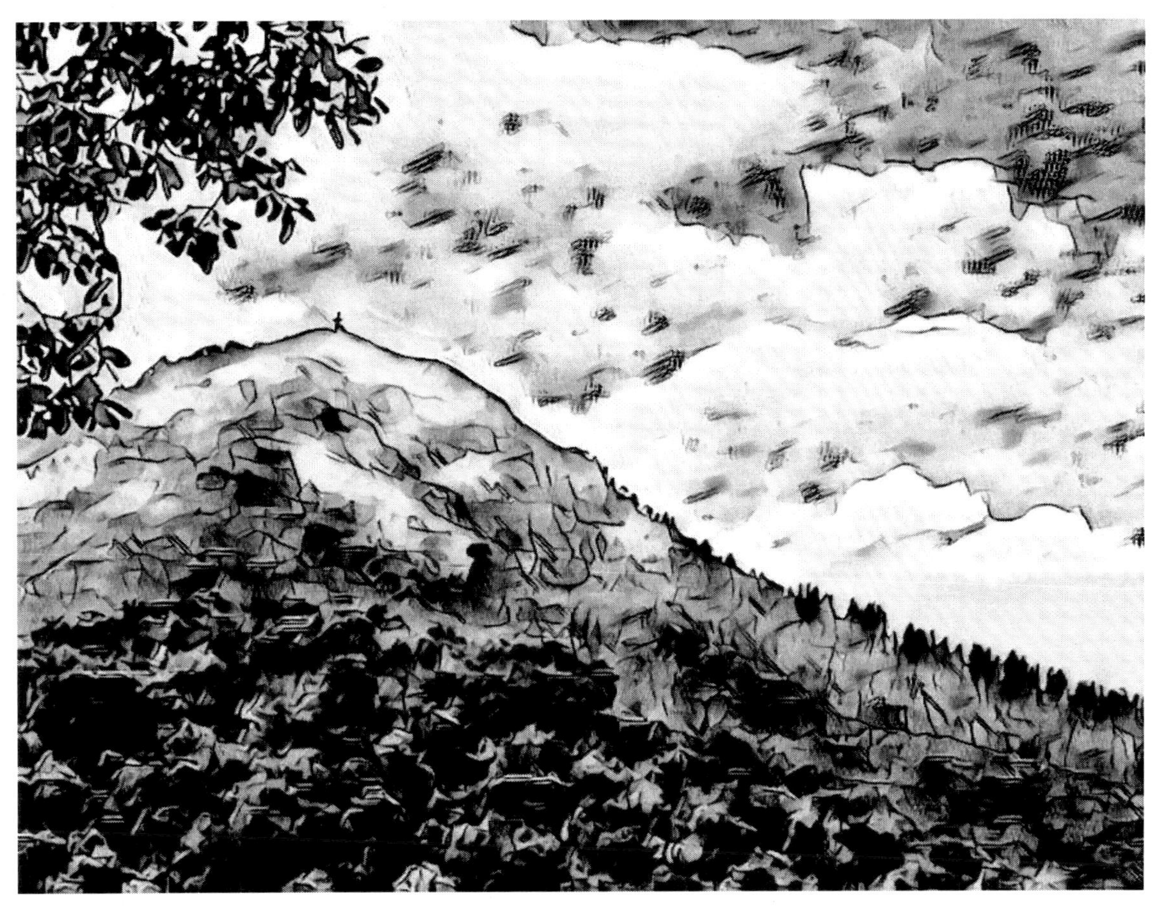

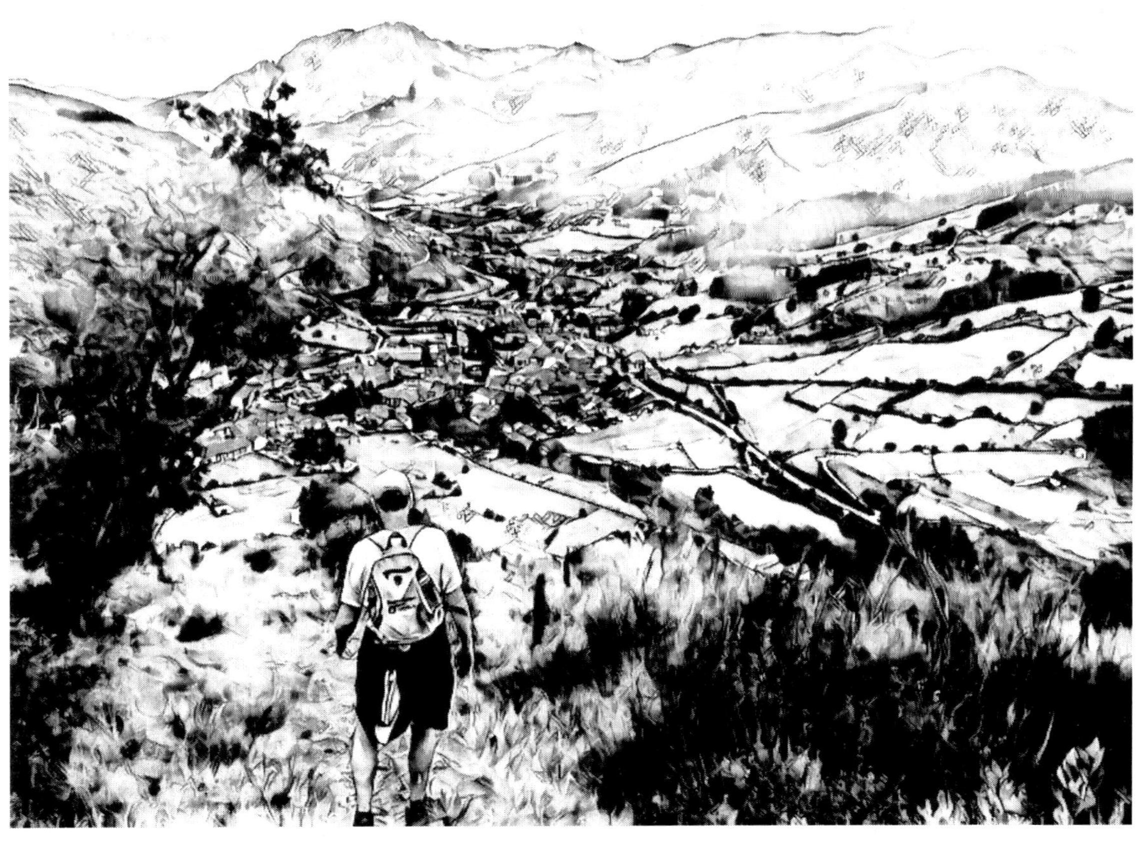

Rio Quiviesa

Hammett/Arana

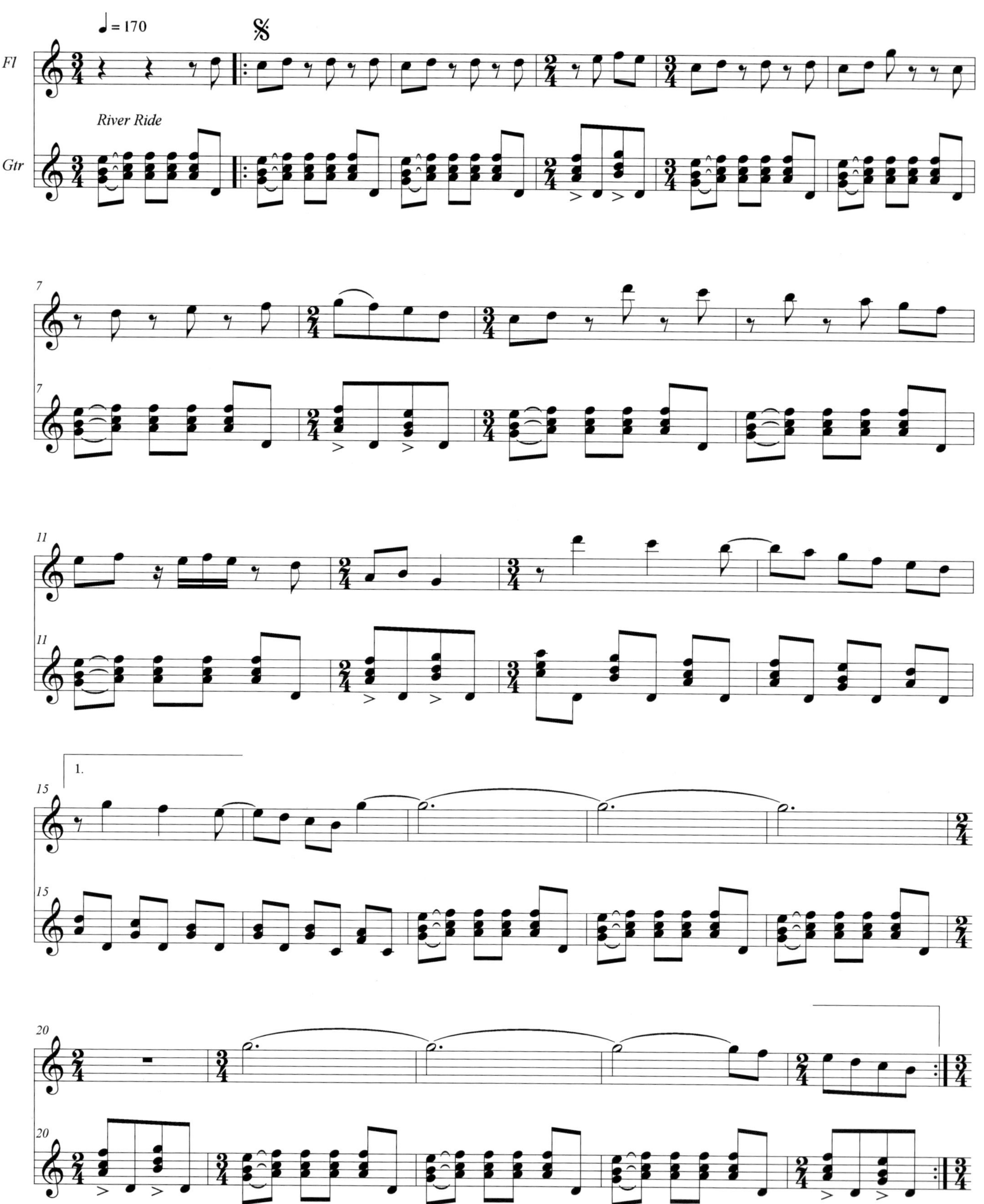

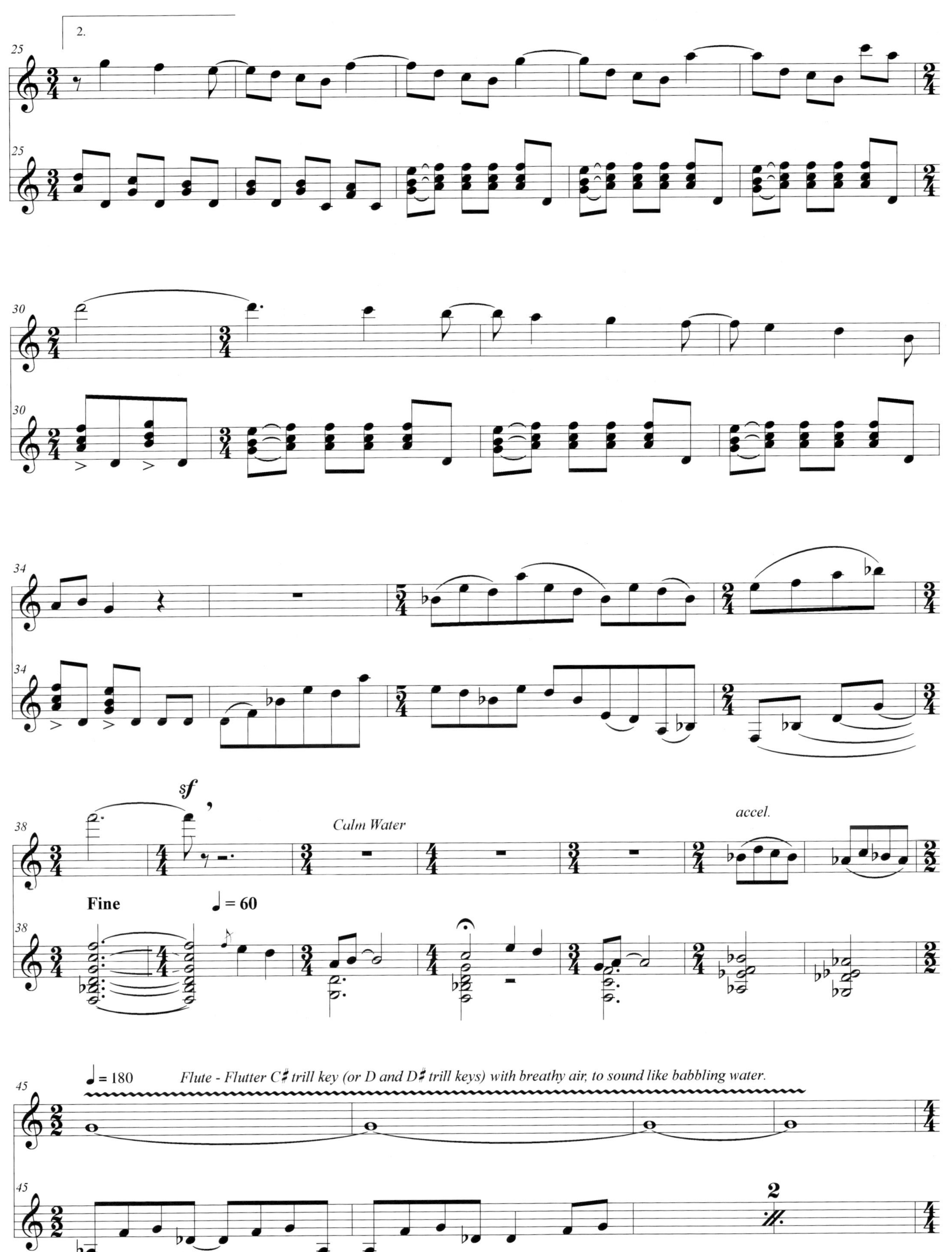
2.
Fine
sf
Calm Water
♩ = 60
accel.
♩ = 180
Flute - Flutter C♯ trill key (or D and D♯ trill keys) with breathy air, to sound like babbling water.

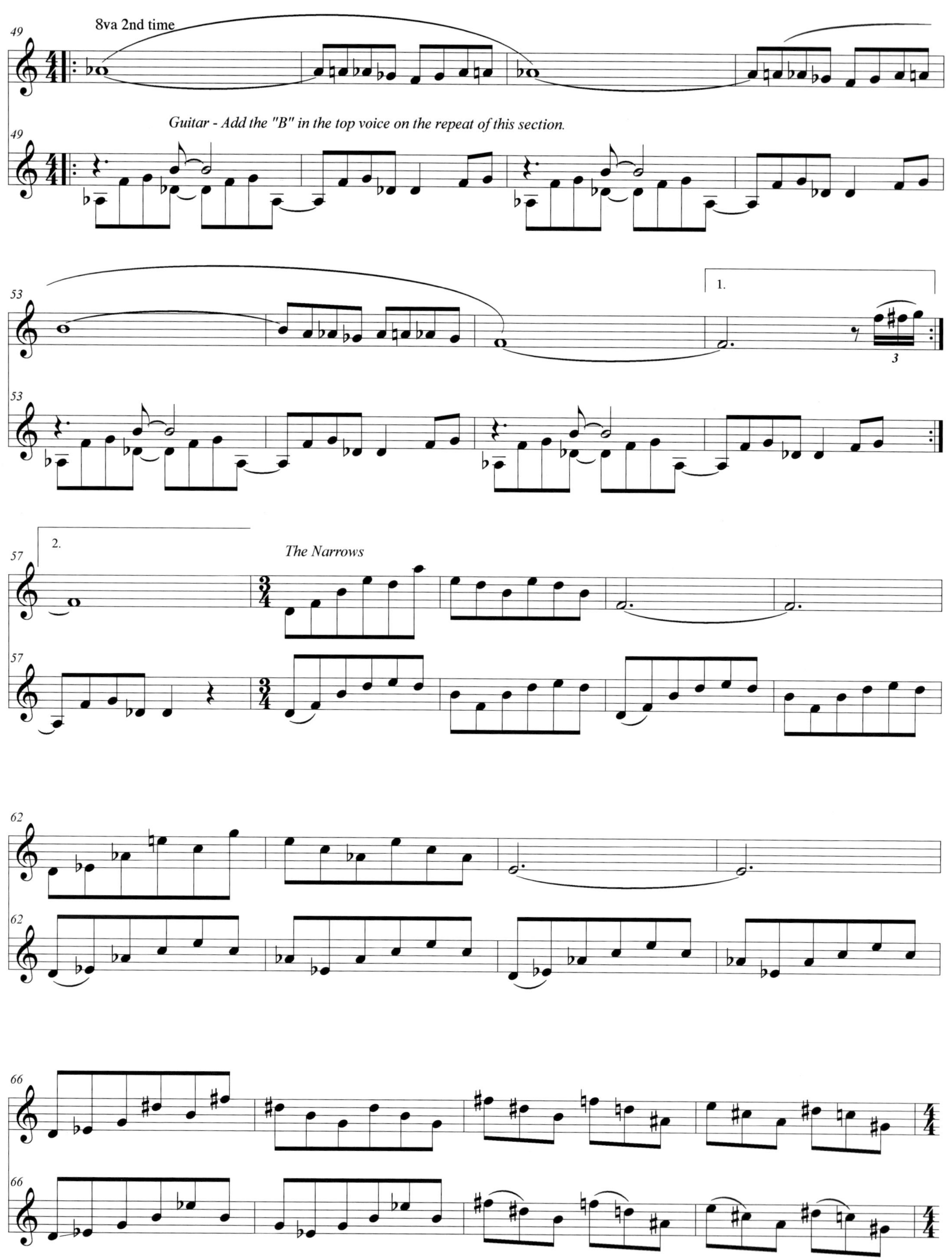
8va 2nd time
Guitar - Add the "B" in the top voice on the repeat of this section.
1.
2.
The Narrows

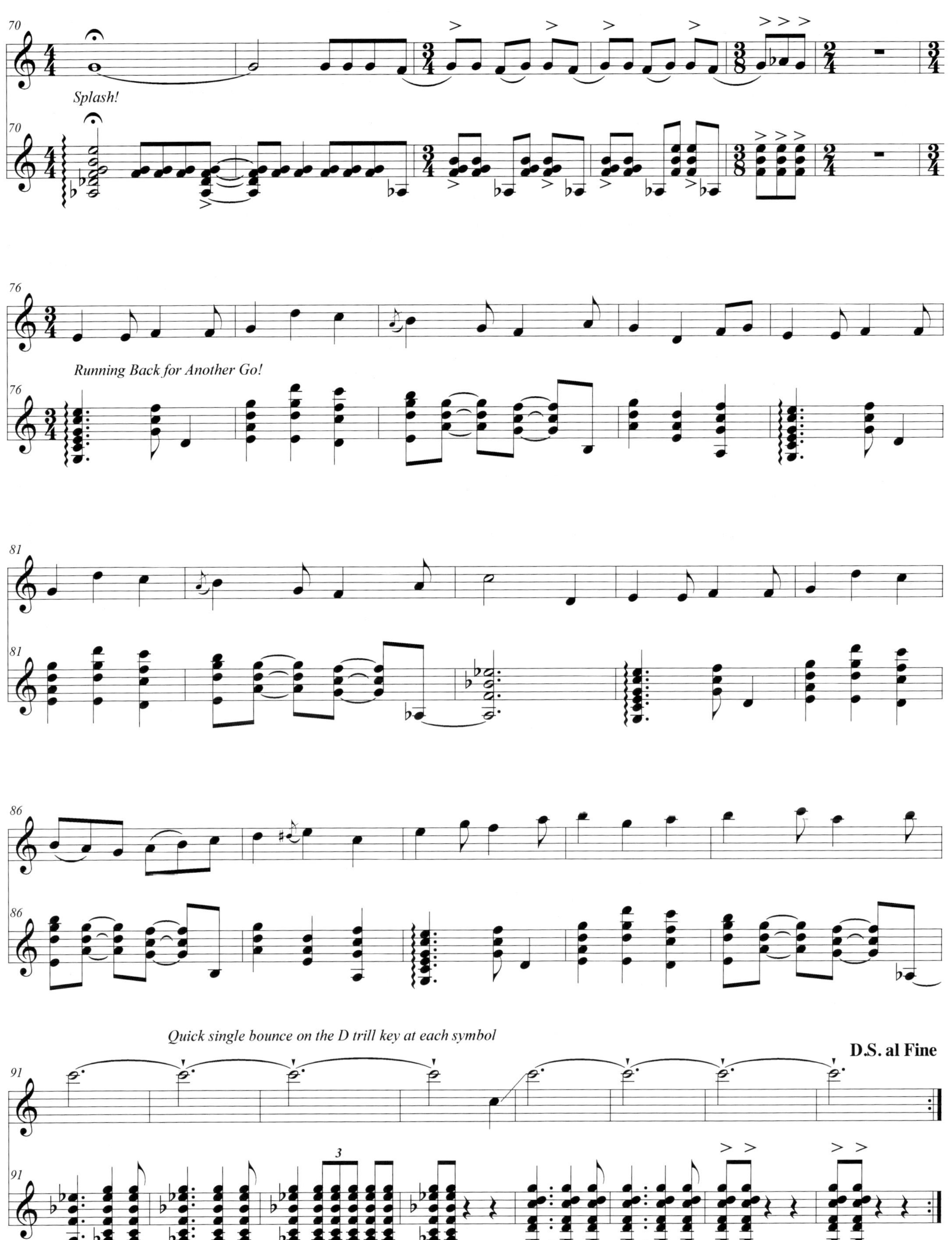
Splash!
Running Back for Another Go!
Quick single bounce on the D trill key at each symbol
D.S. al Fine

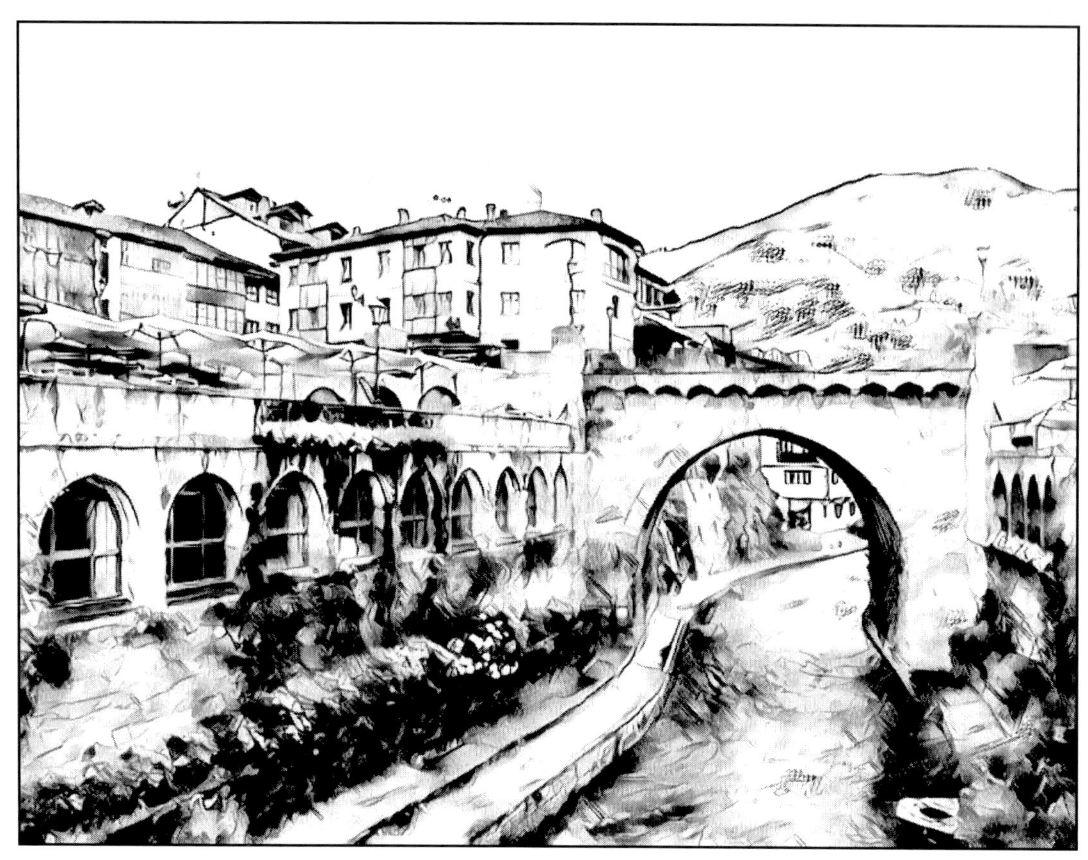

Rio Quiviesa flowing under the San Cayetano Bridge in Potes, Spain

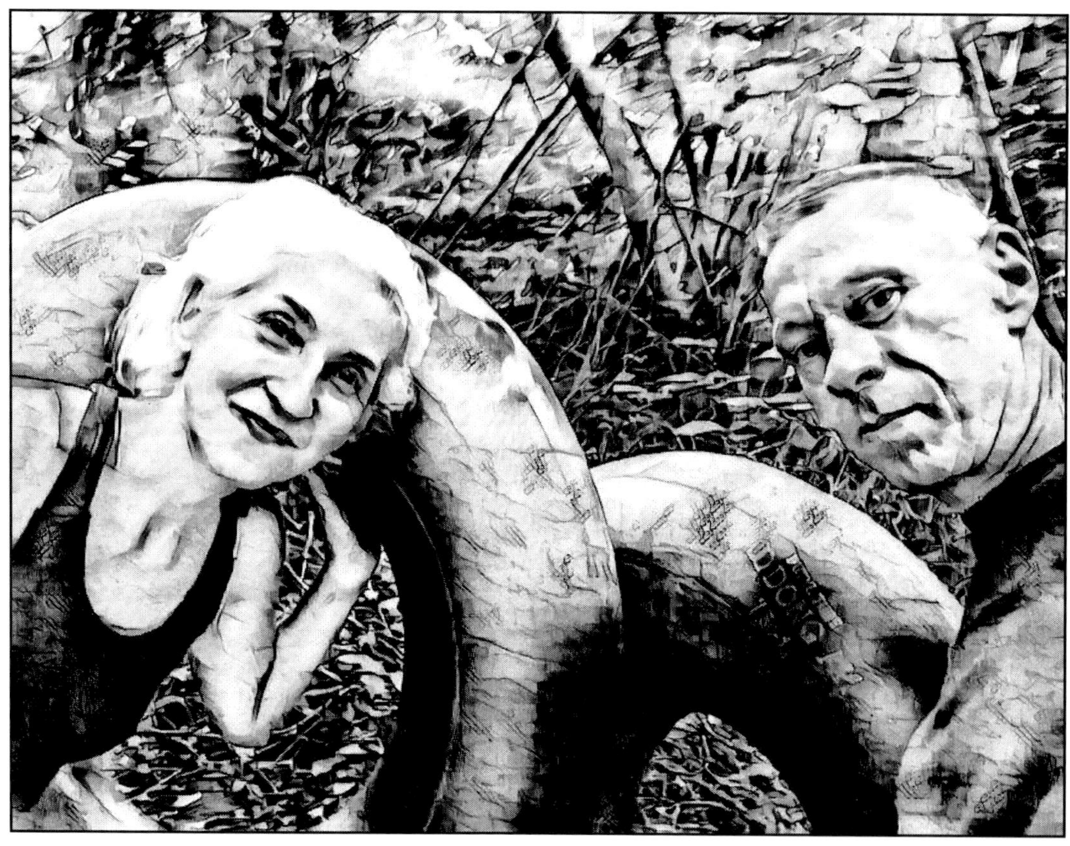

The composers preparing to explore Rio Quiviesa with inner tubes

Monasterio de Santo Toribio

Hammett/Arana

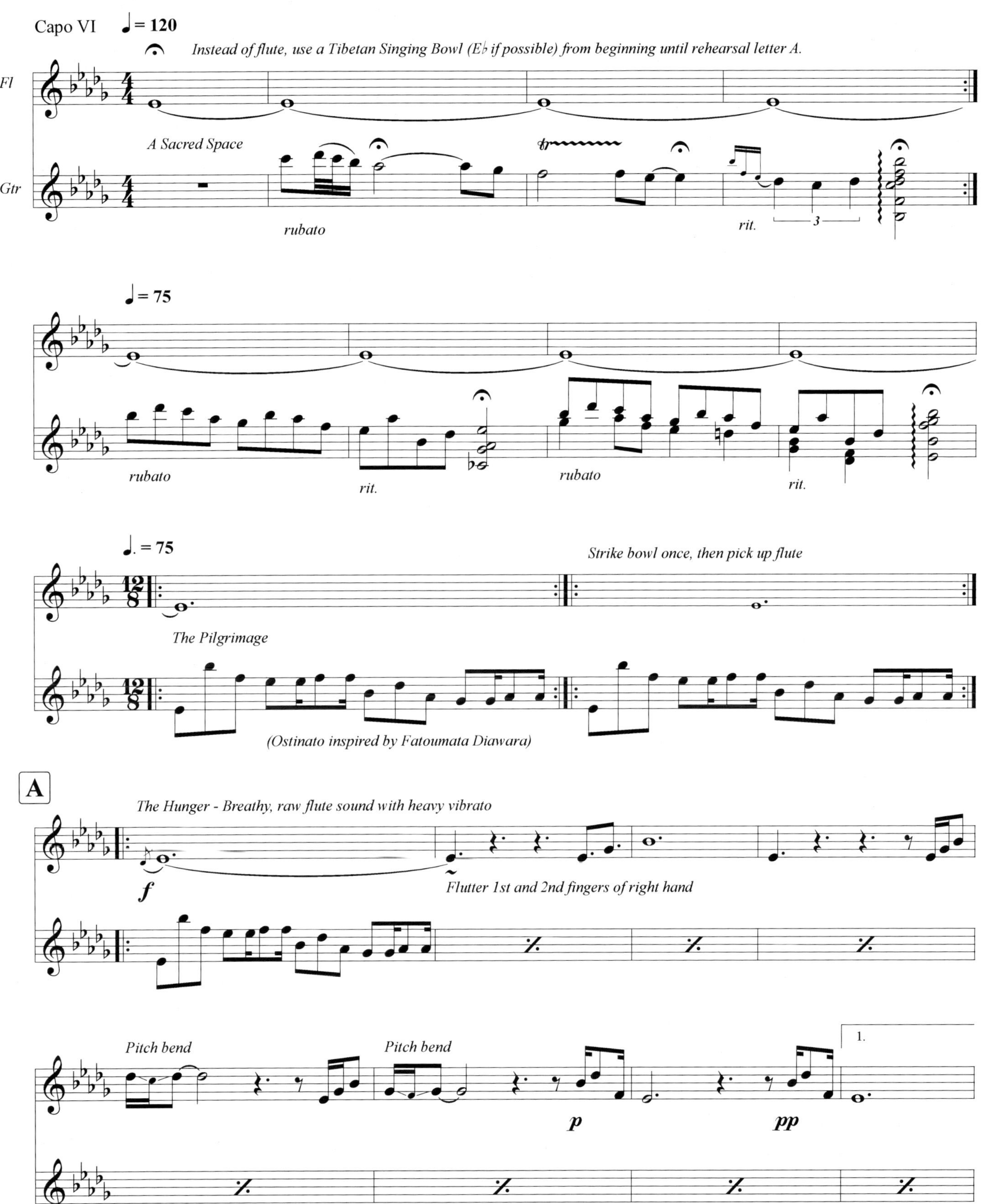

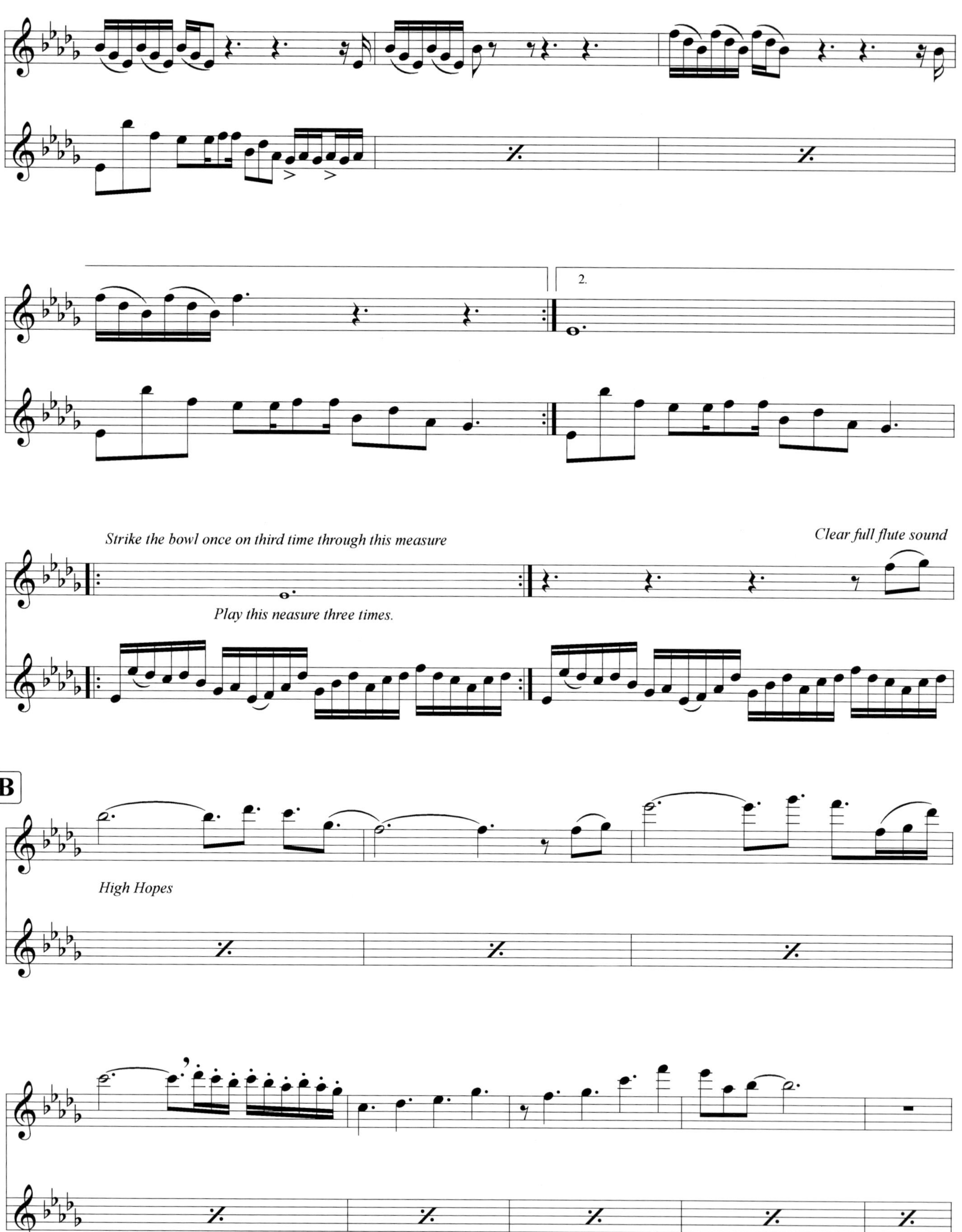
2.
Strike the bowl once on third time through this measure
Play this measure three times.
Clear full flute sound
B
High Hopes

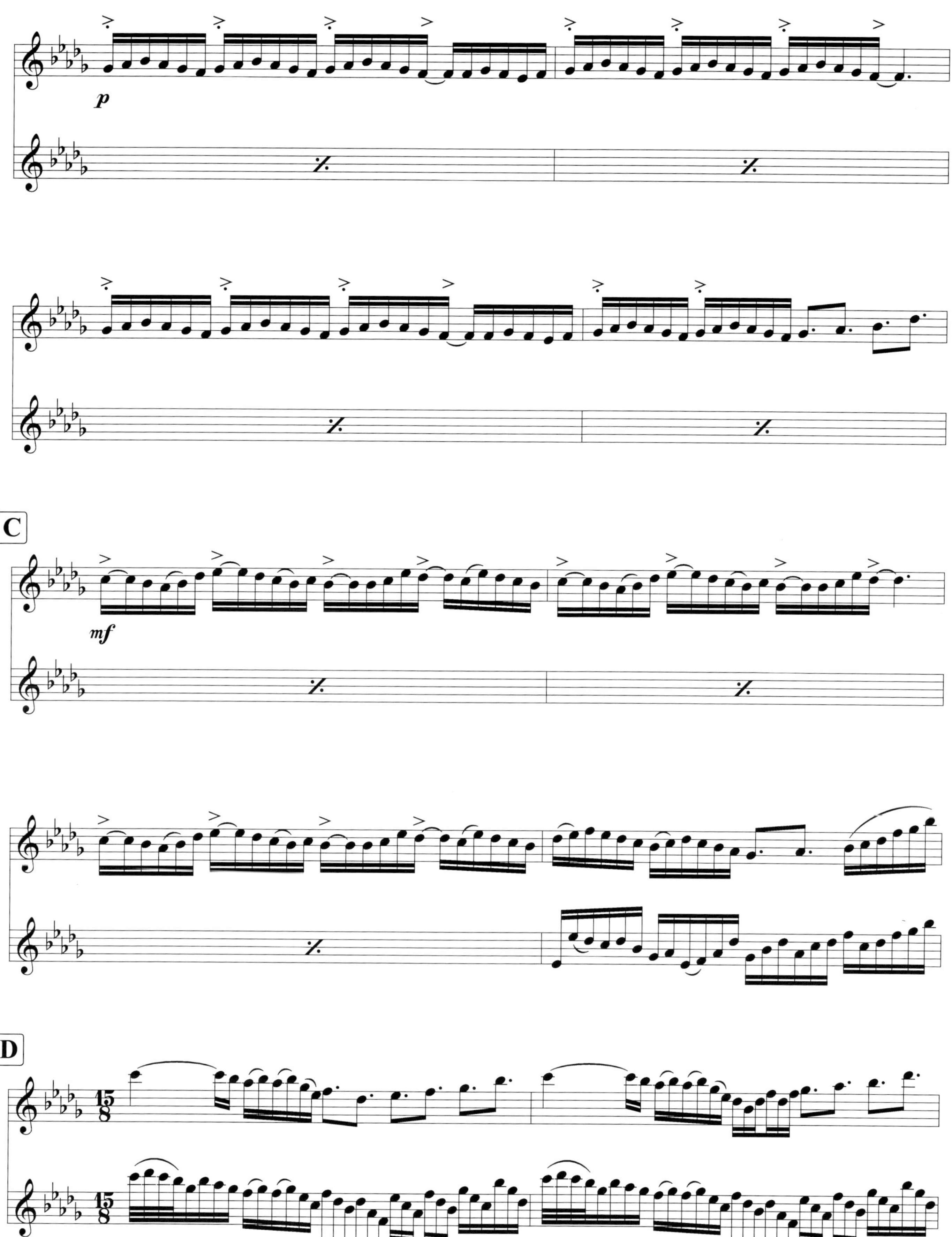
p
C
mf
D
15
8

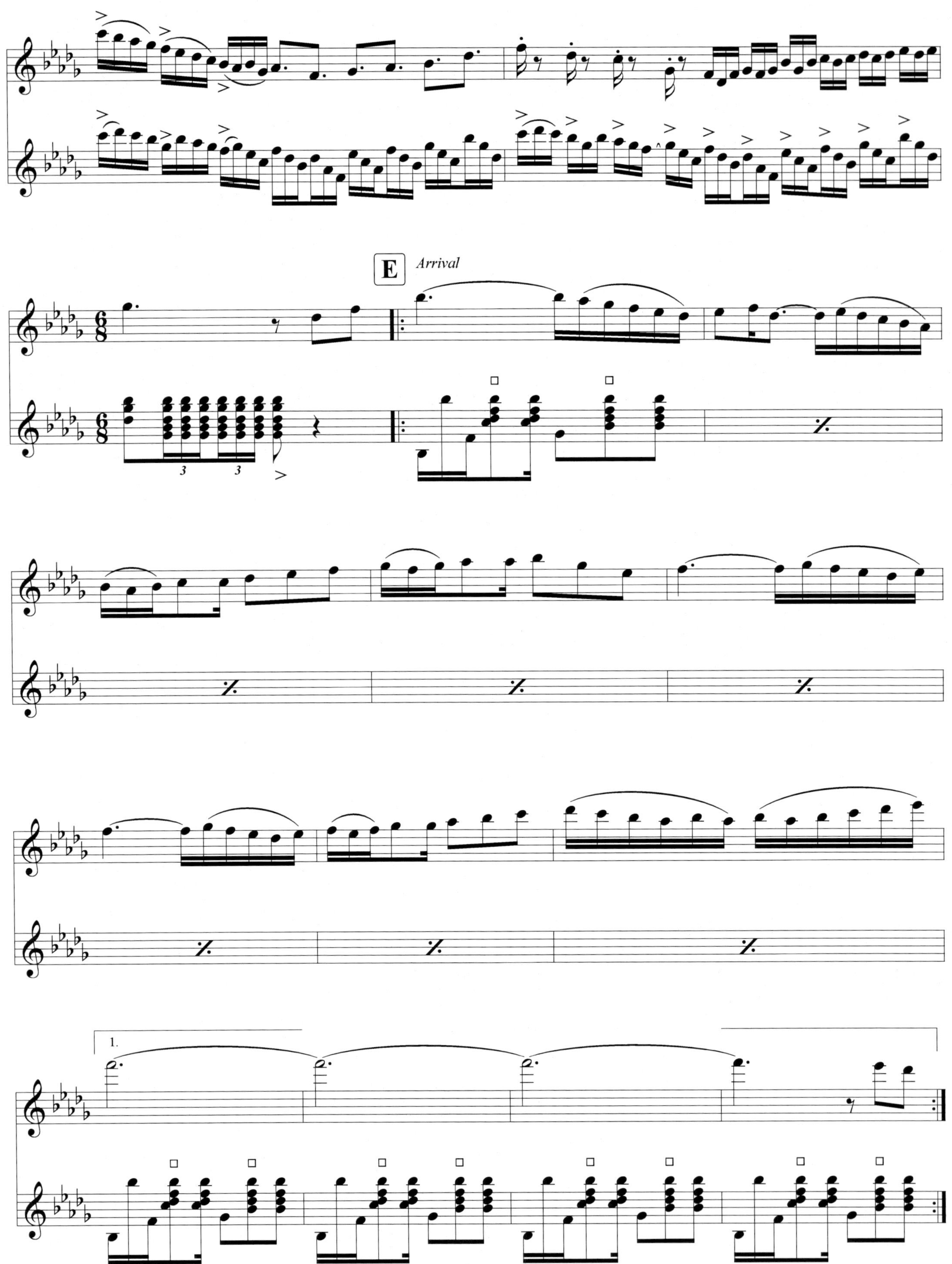
E
Arrival
3
3
1.

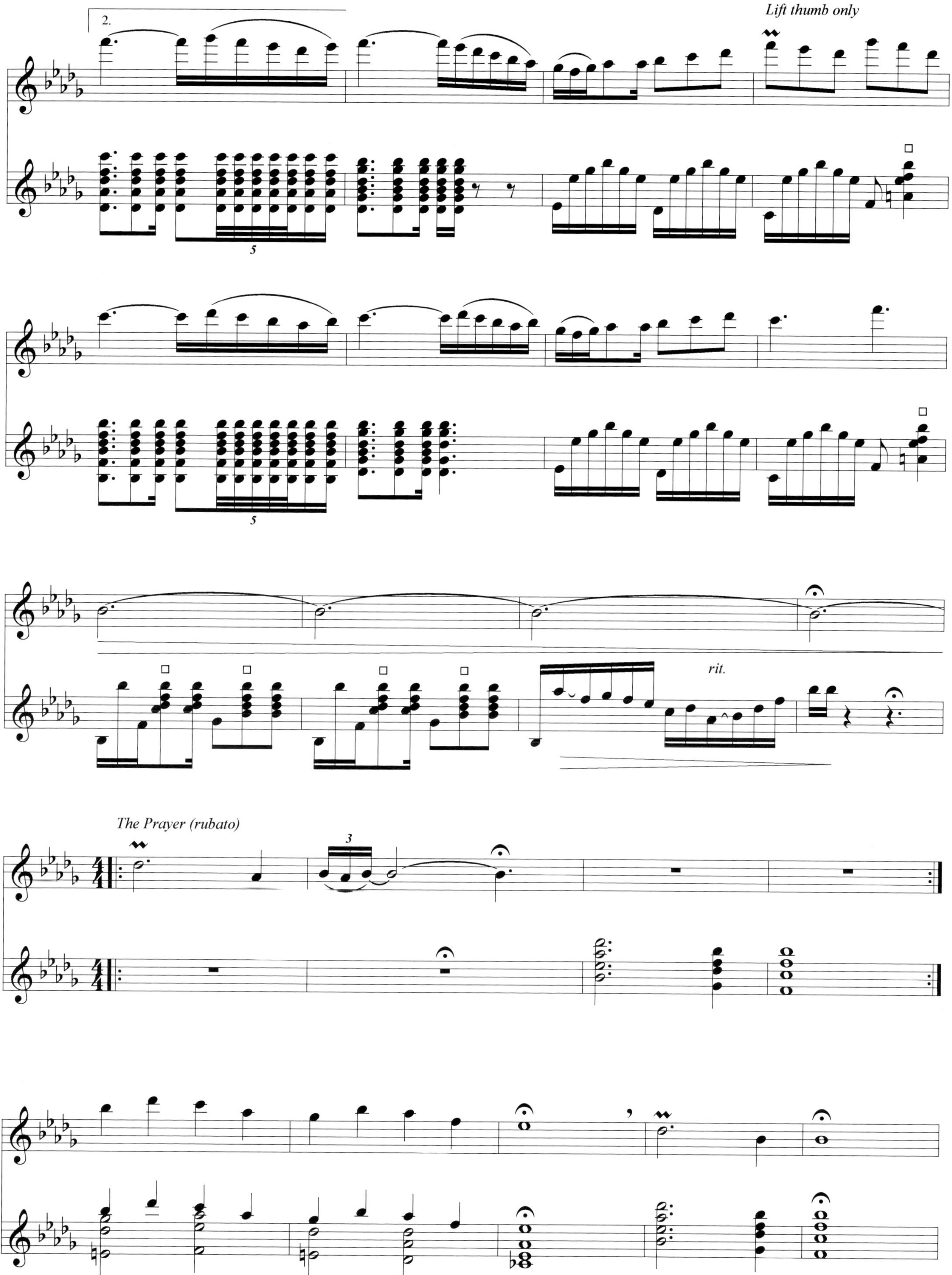
2.
Lift thumb only
5
5
rit.
The Prayer (rubato)
3

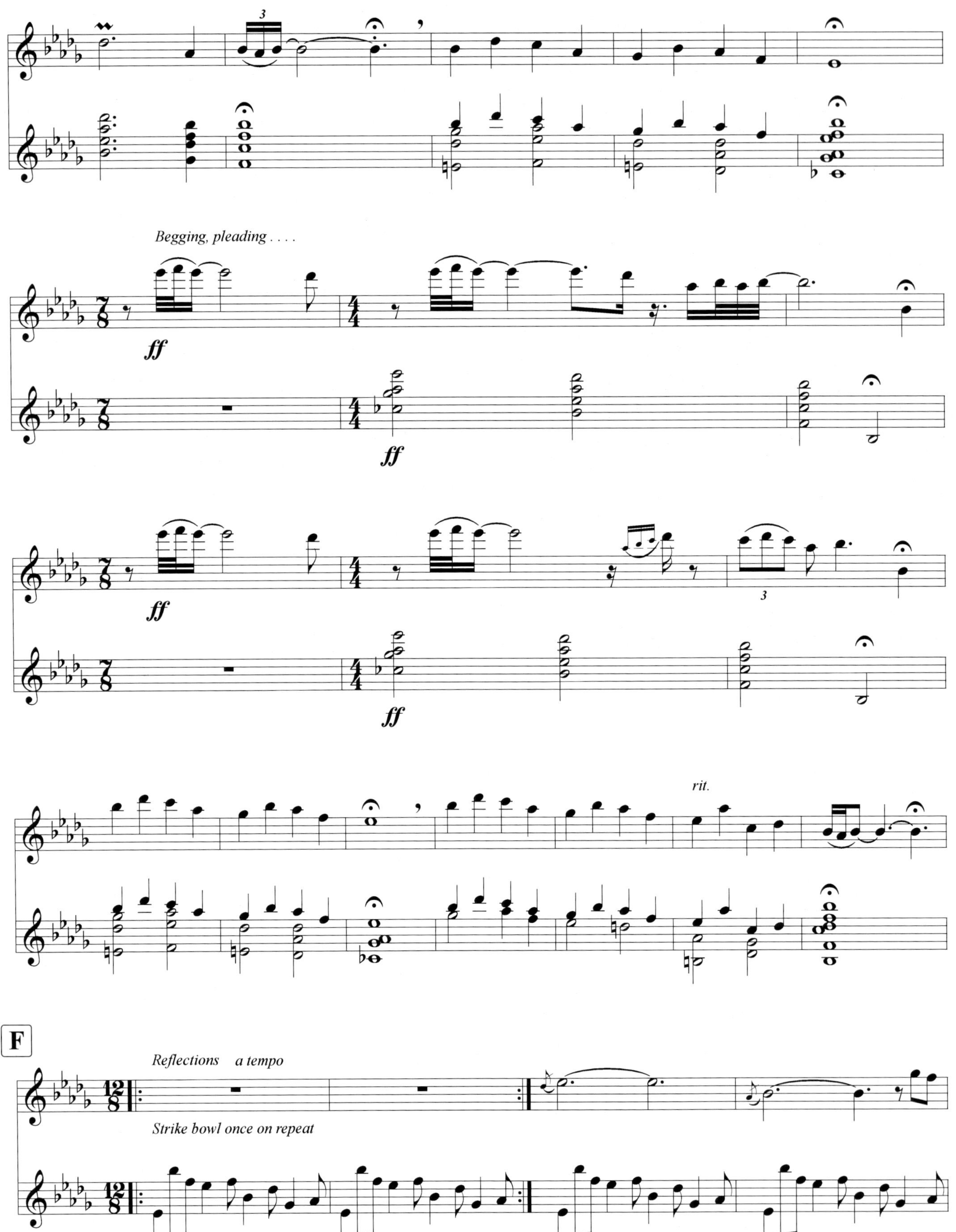
Begging, pleading . . . .
ff
ff
ff
ff
rit.
F
Reflections a tempo
Strike bowl once on repeat

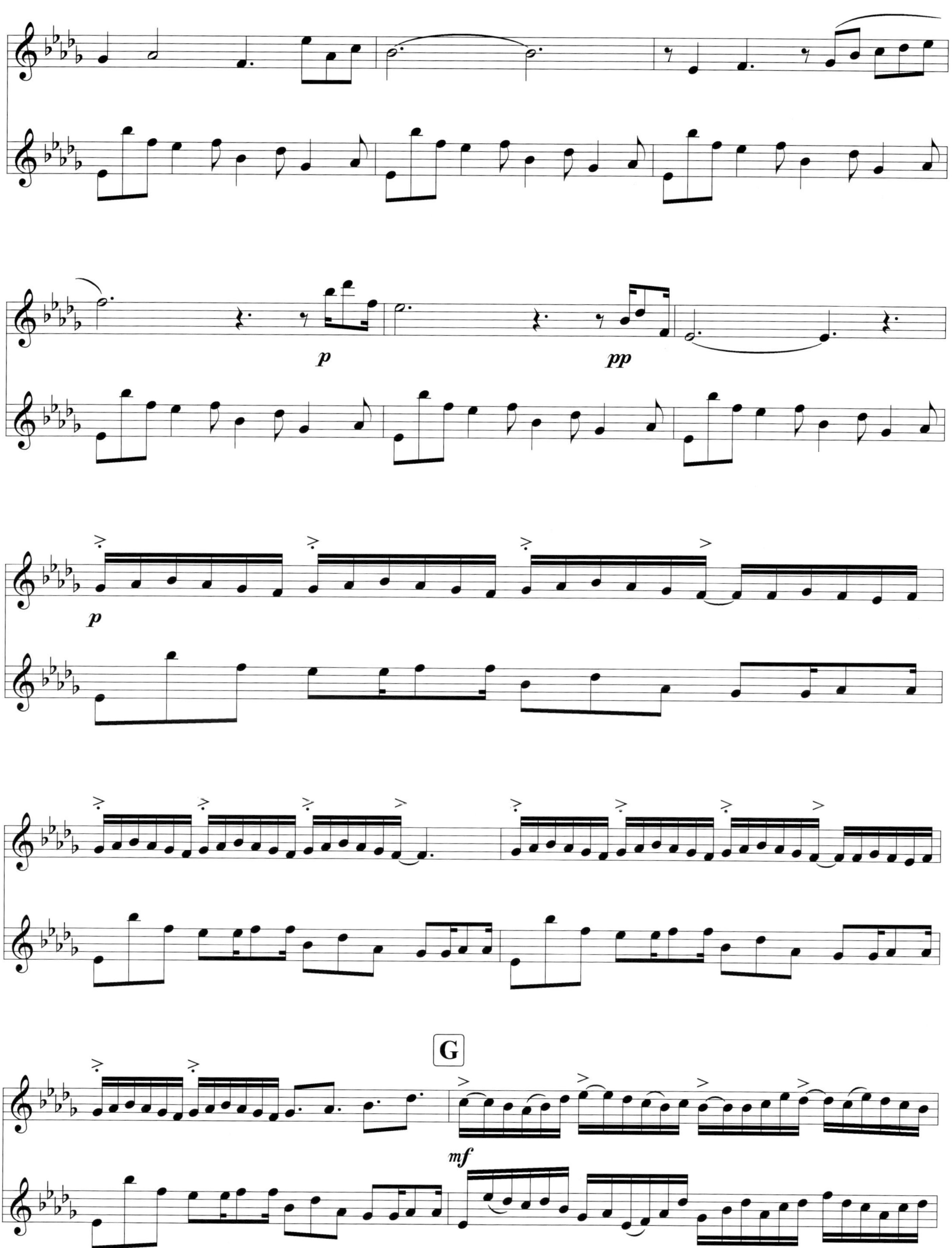
p
pp
p
G
mf

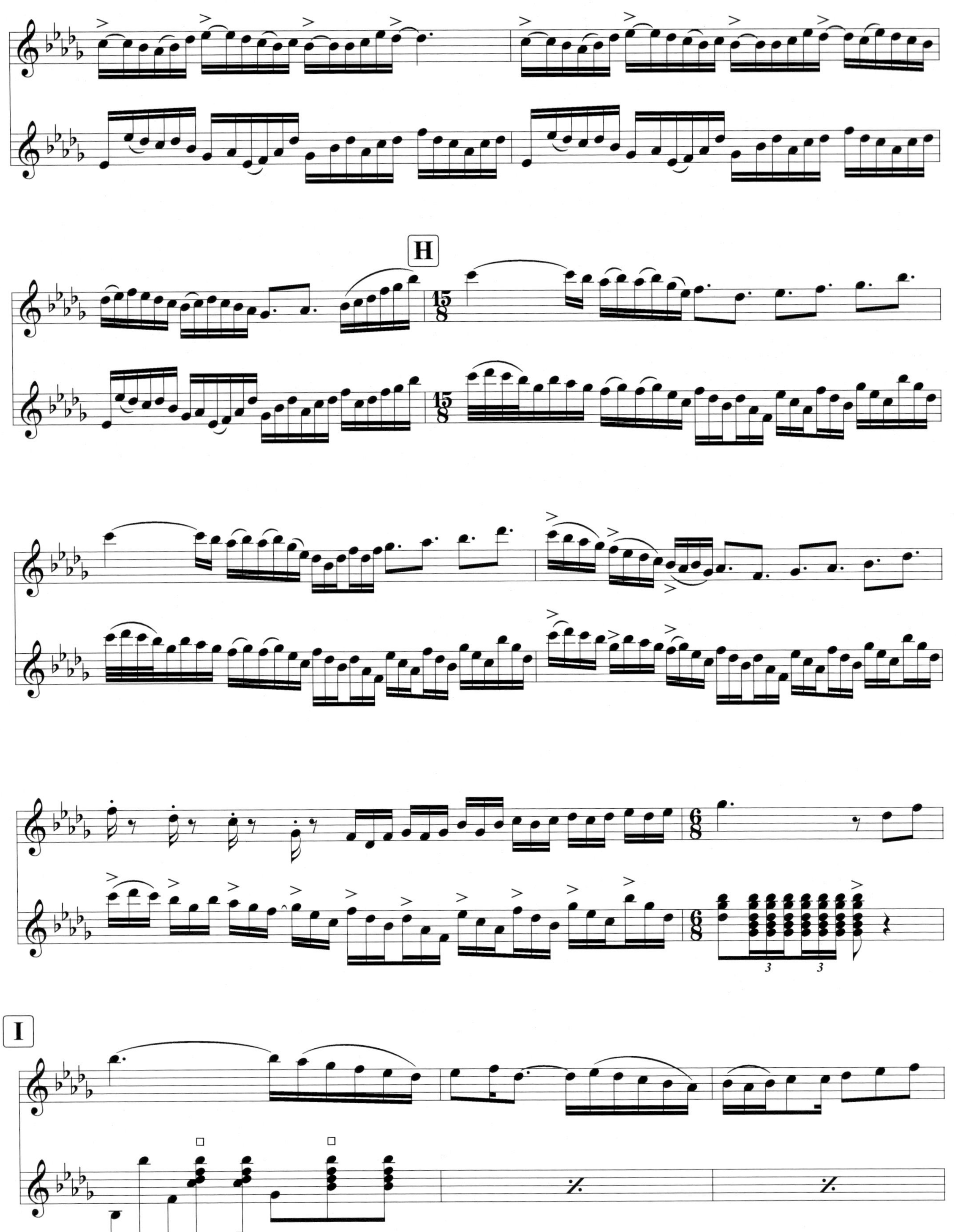
H
15
8
15
8
6
8
6
8
3
3
I

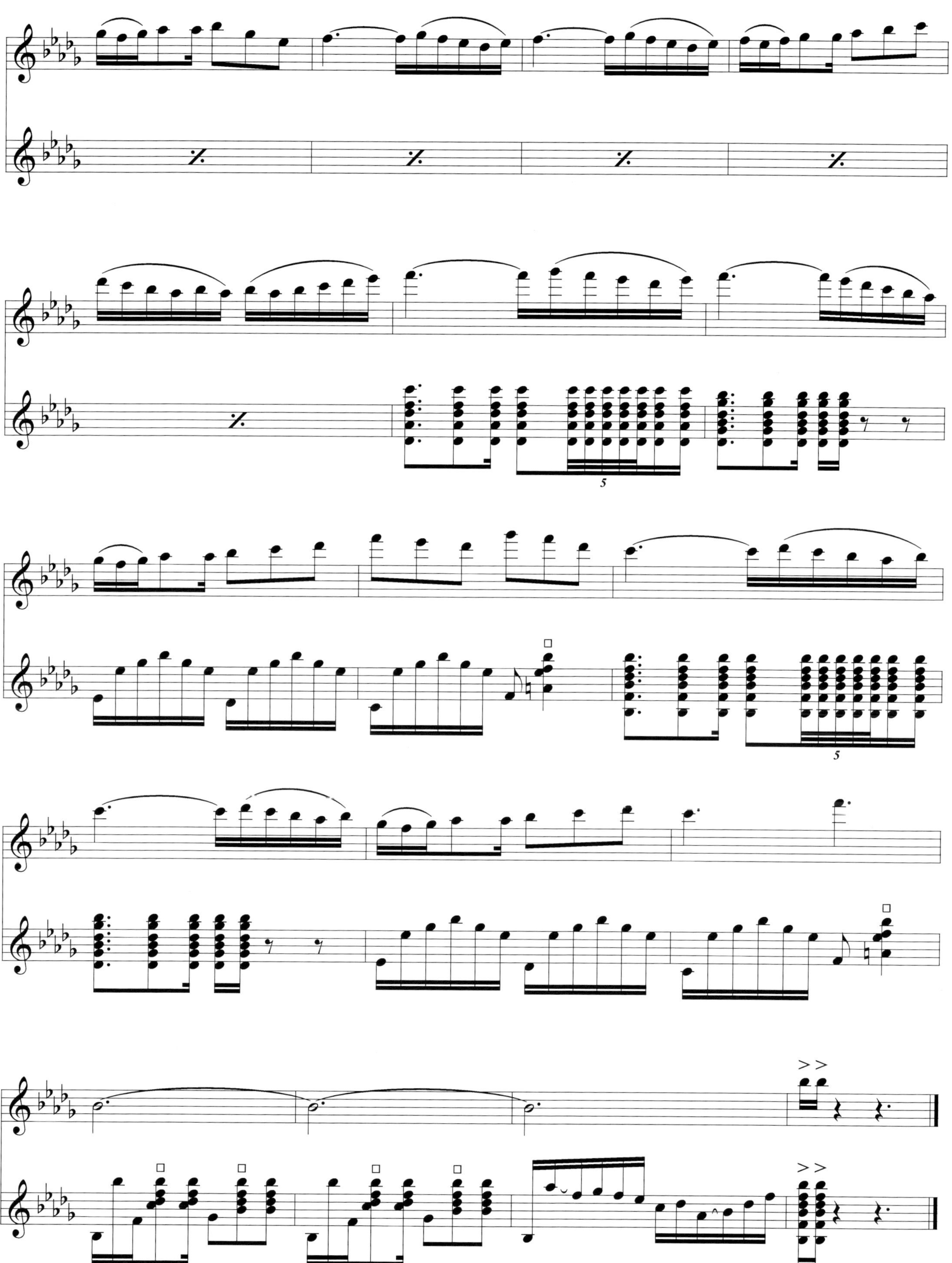

Monasterio de Santo Toribio, Potes, Spain

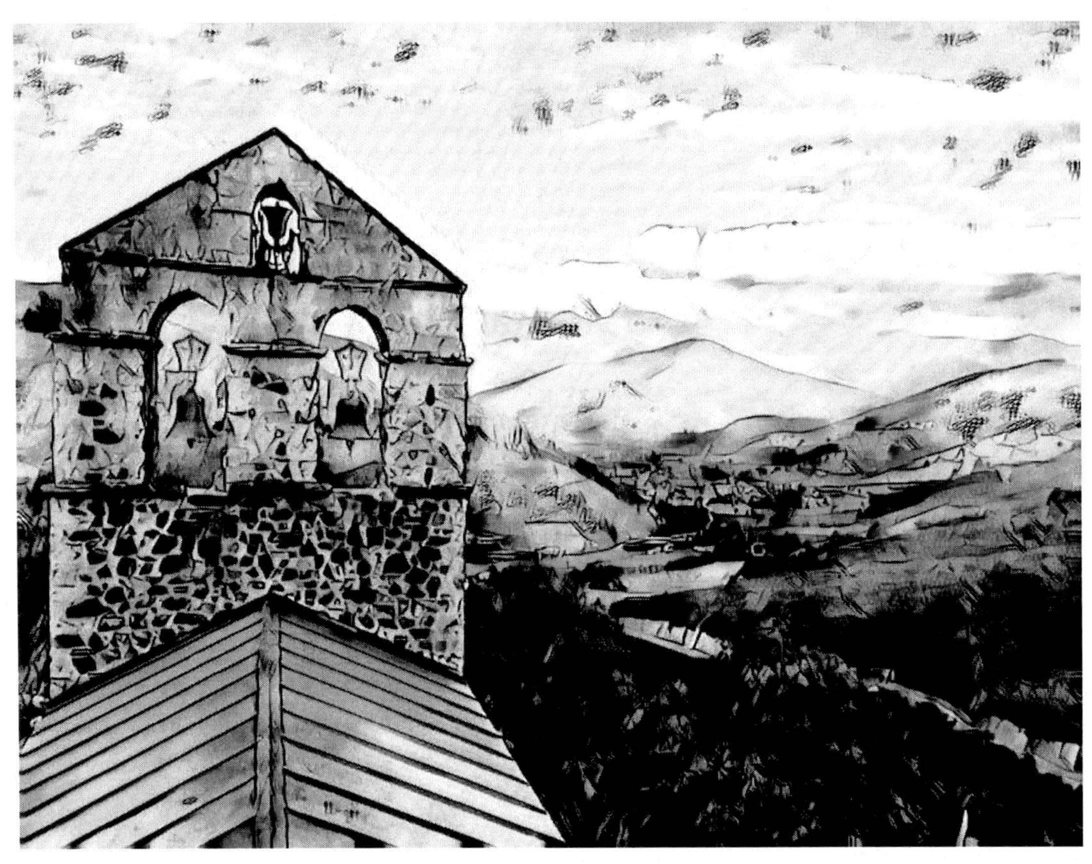

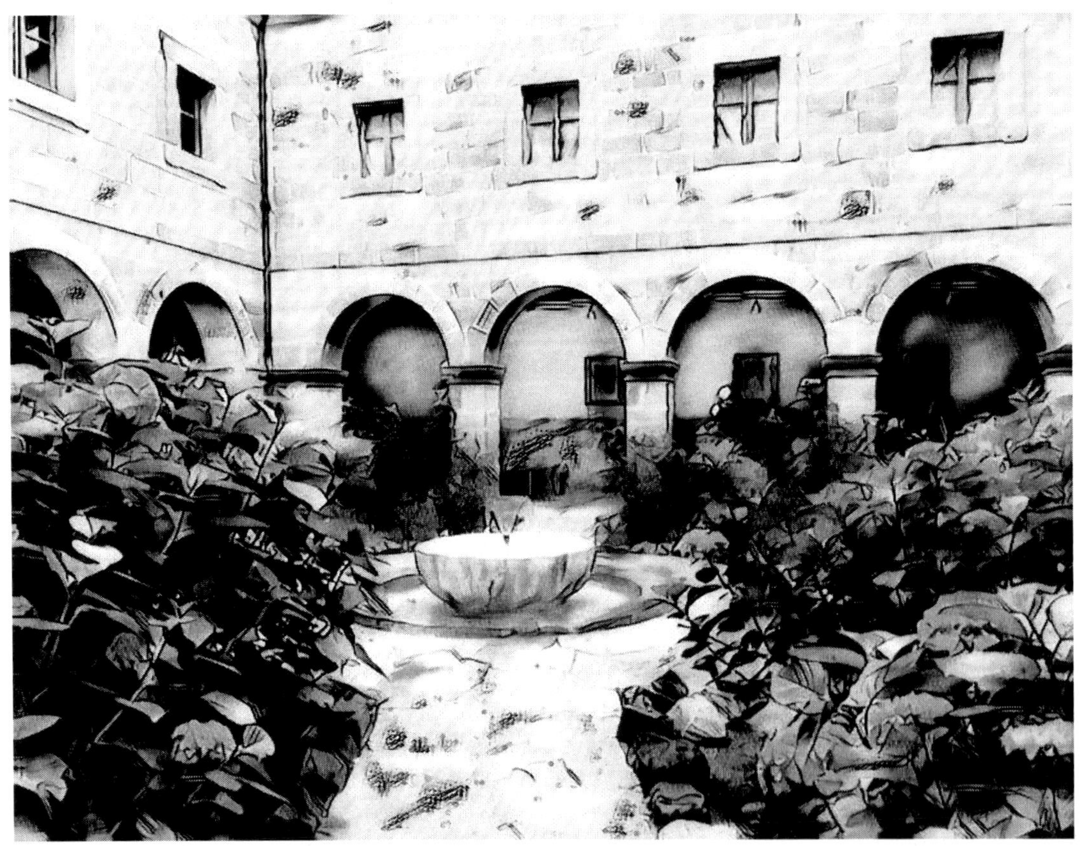

Retratos de Potes

Hammett/Arana

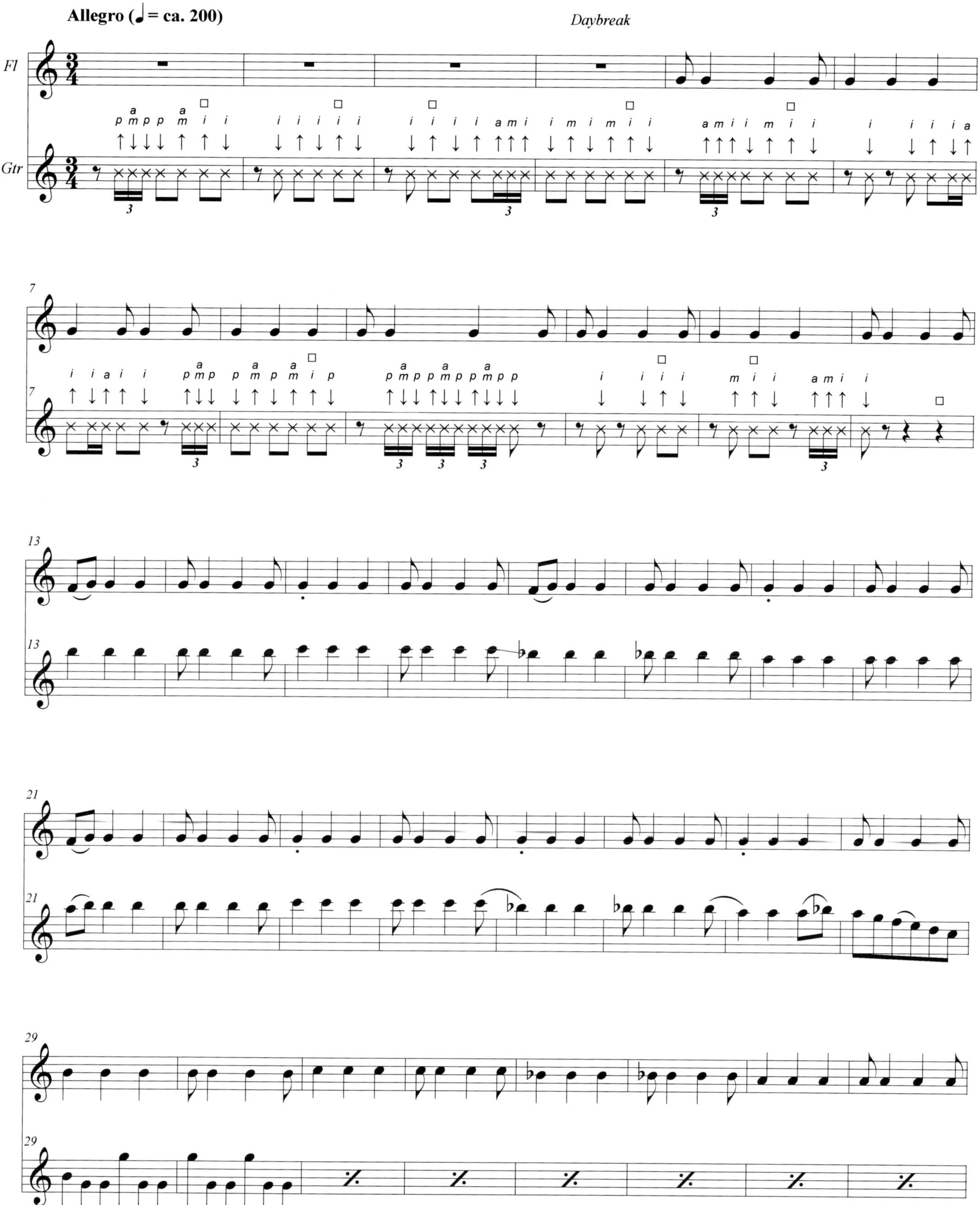

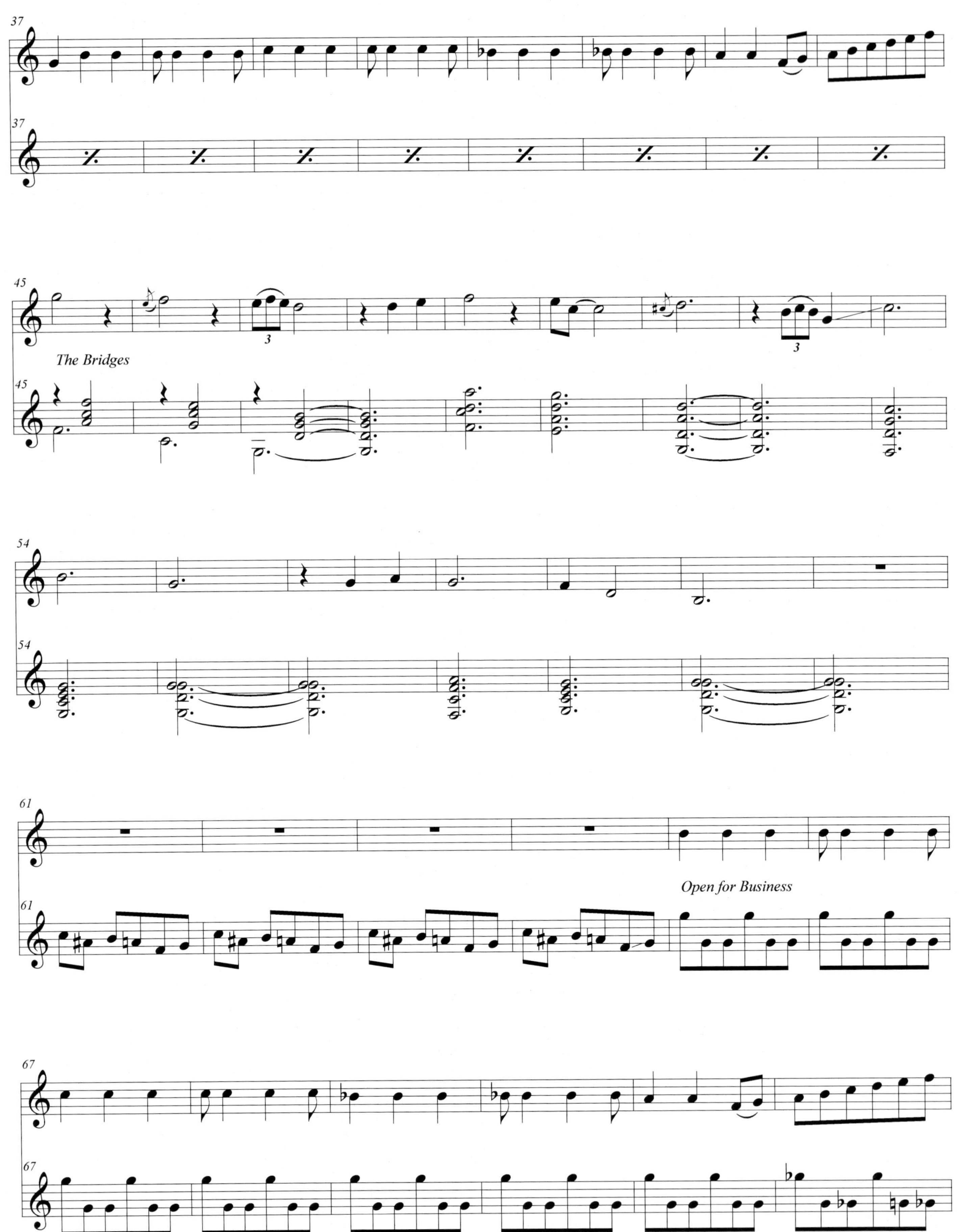
The Bridges
Open for Business

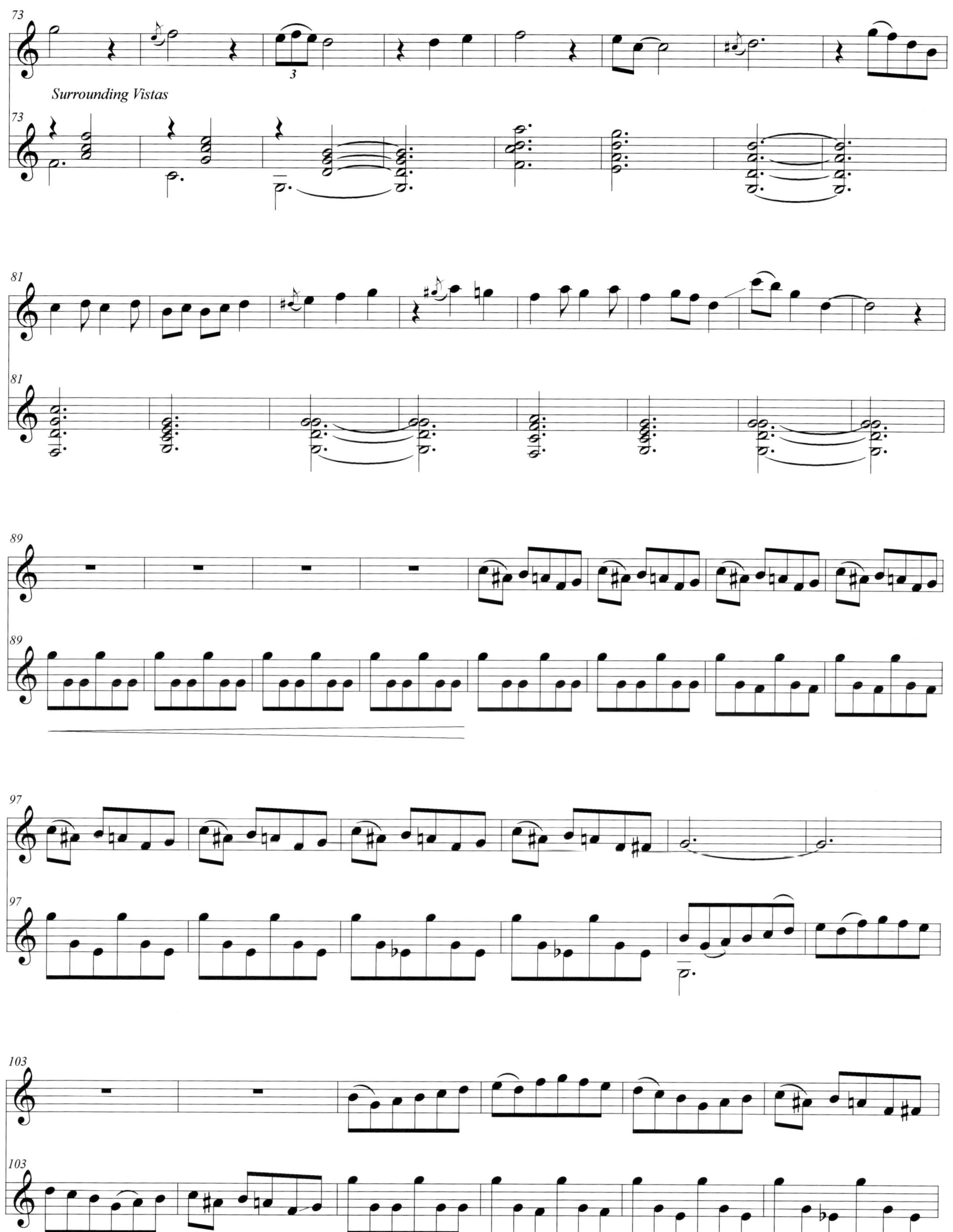
73
Surrounding Vistas
3
81
89
97
103

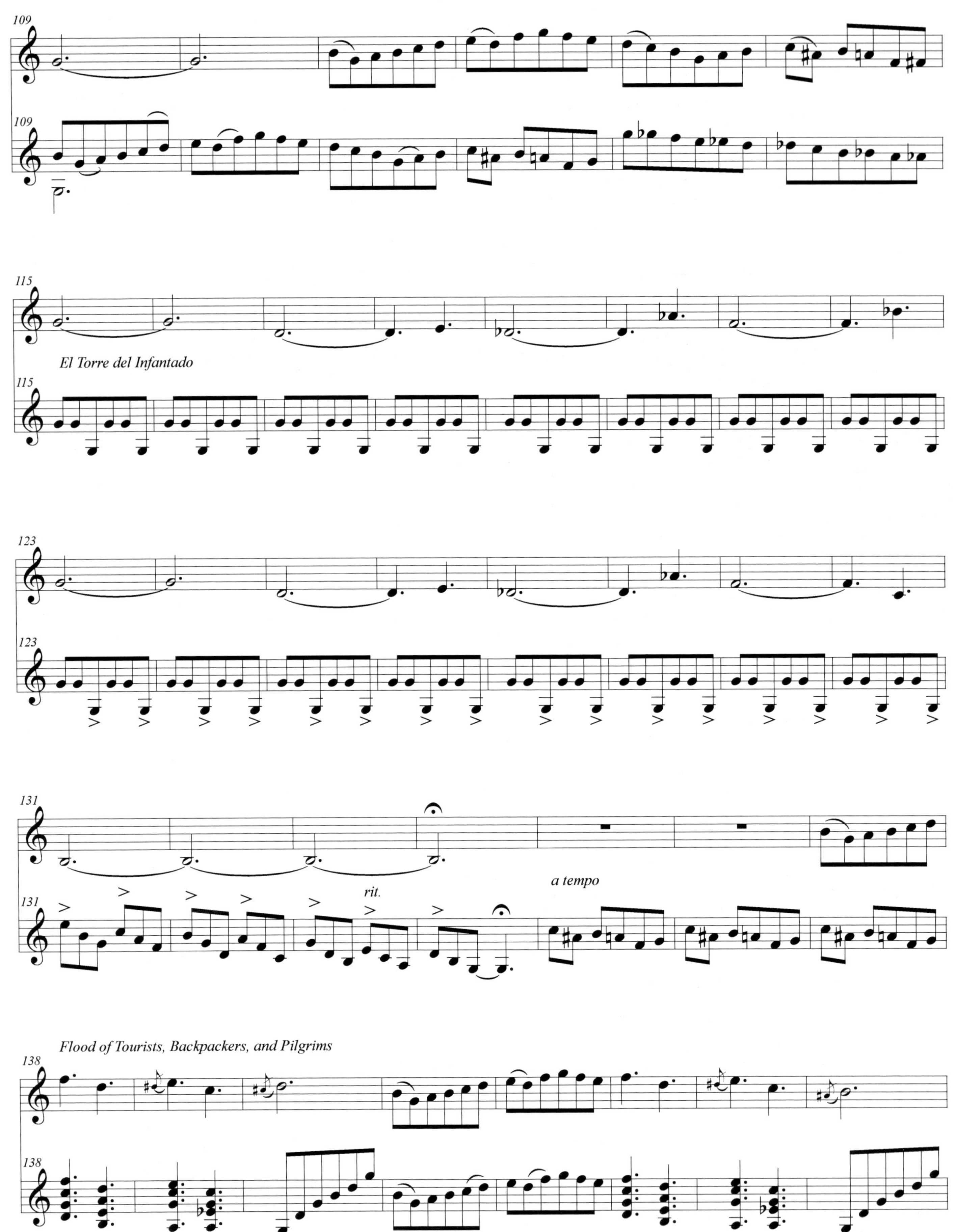
109
109
115
El Torre del Infantado
115
123
123
131
a tempo
131
rit.
Flood of Tourists, Backpackers, and Pilgrims
138
138

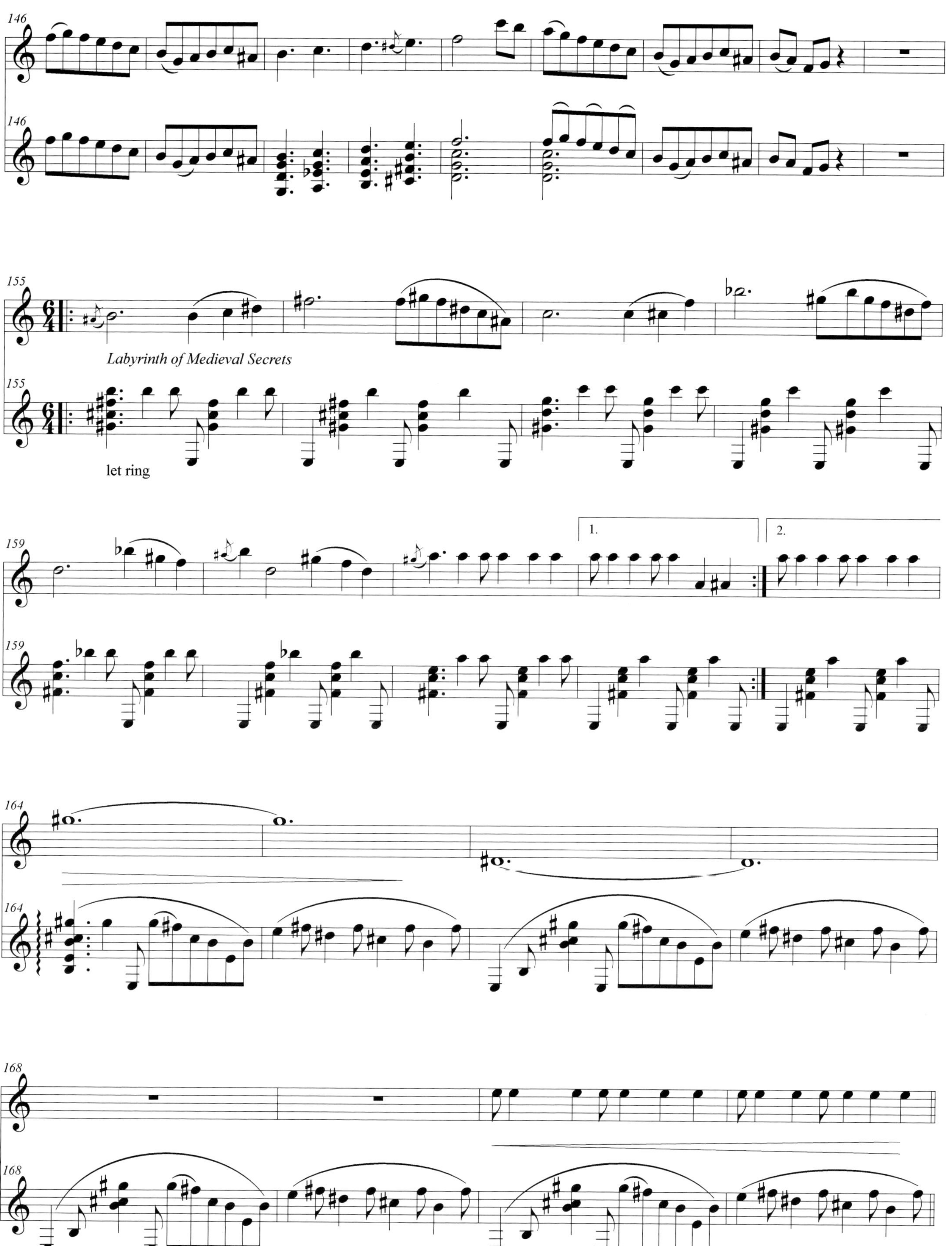
Labyrinth of Medieval Secrets
let ring
1.
2.

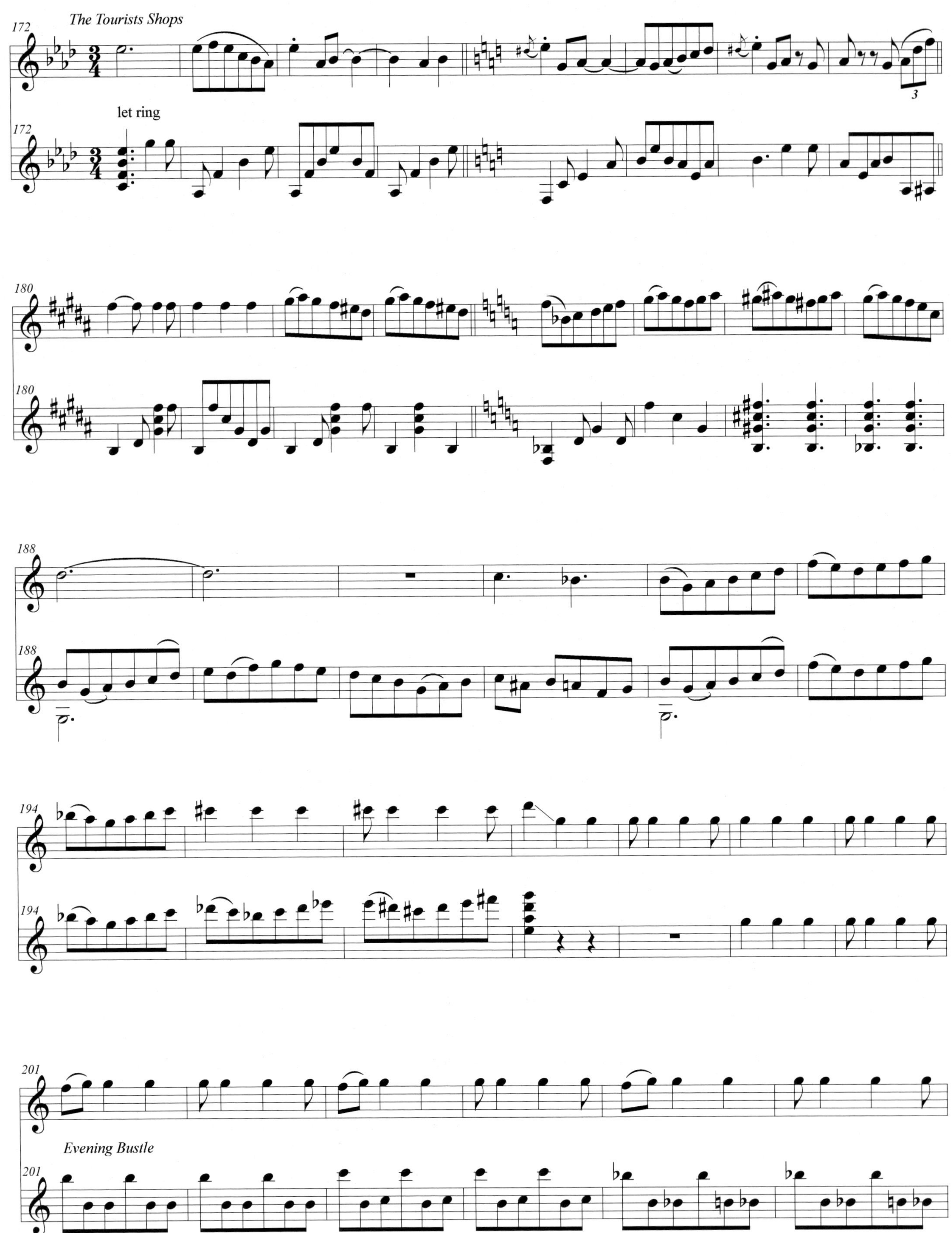
172
The Tourists Shops
3
172
let ring
180
180
188
188
194
194
201
Evening Bustle
201

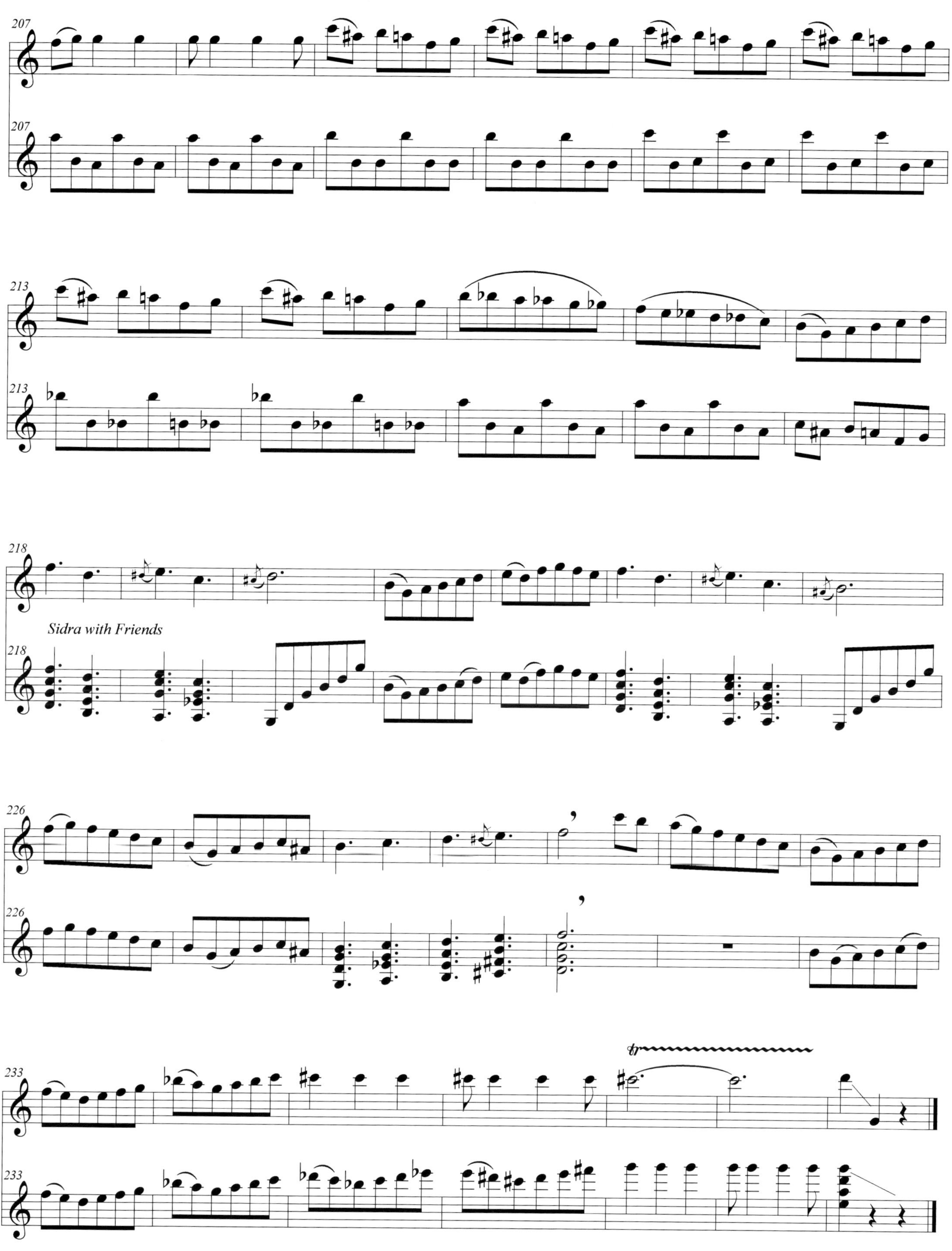
207
207
213
213
218
Sidra with Friends
218
226
226
233
233
tr

The village of Potes in Northern Spain

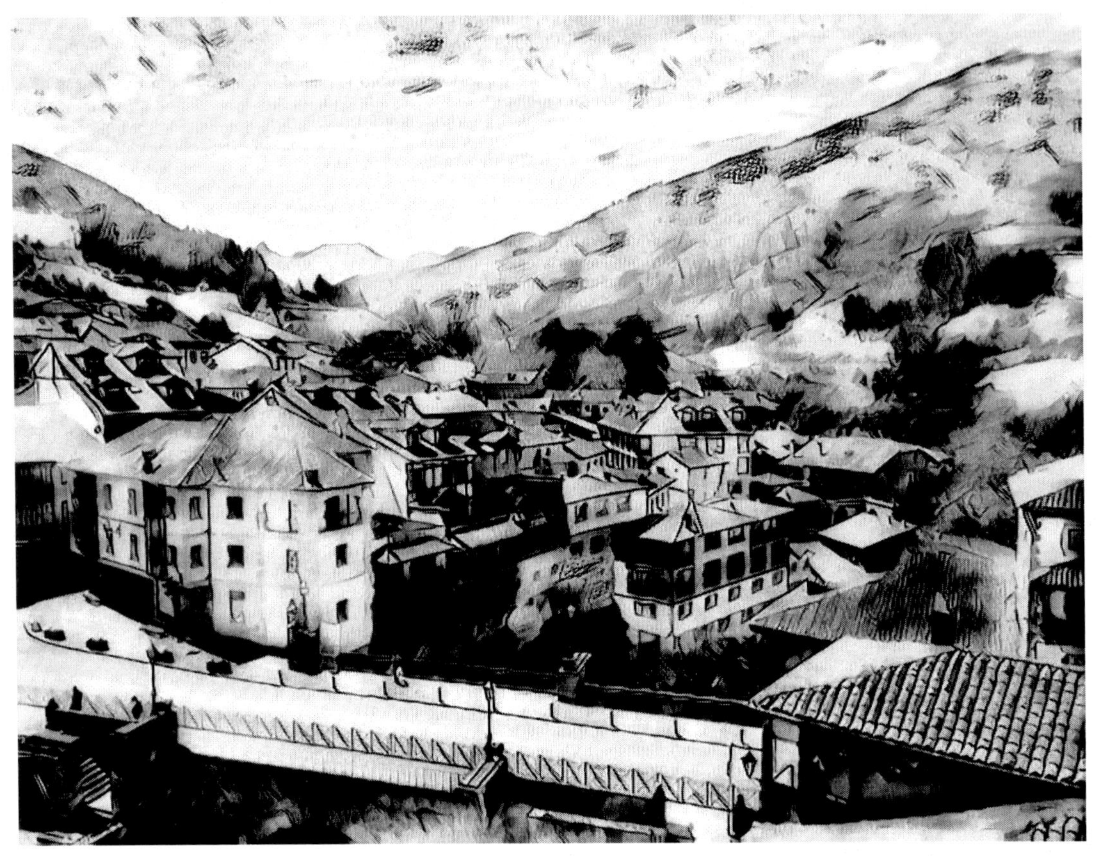

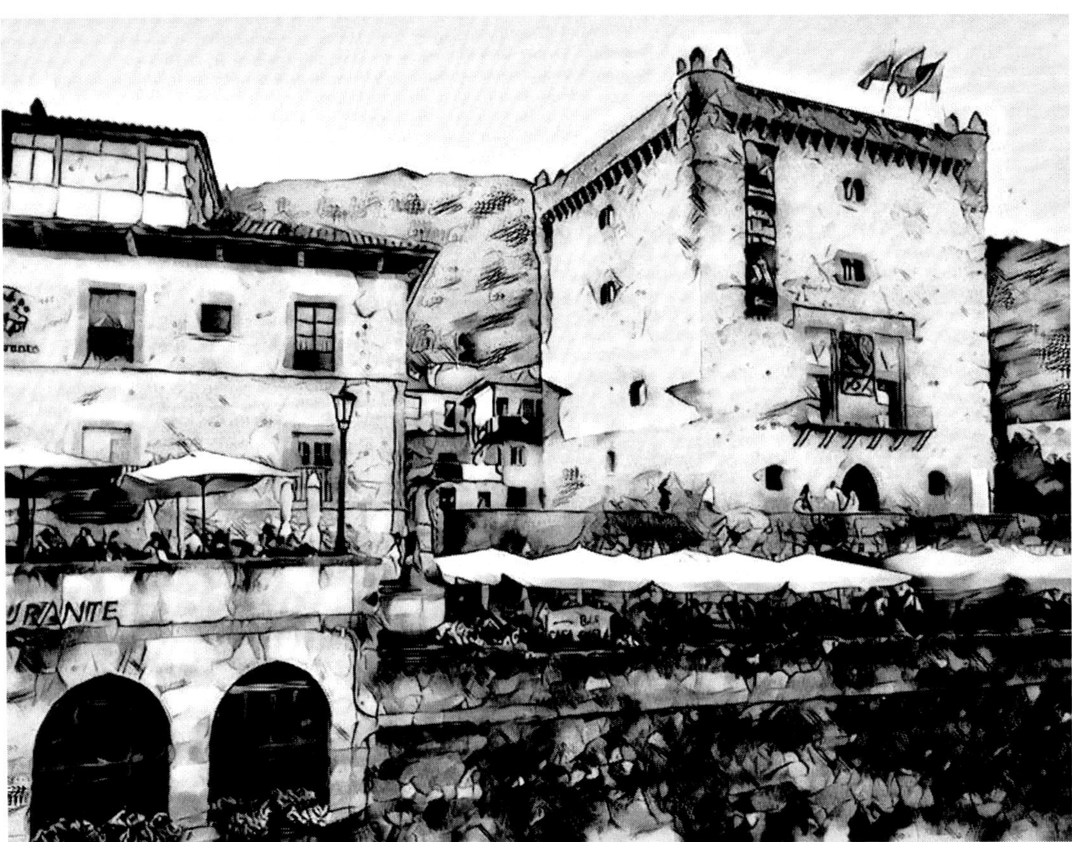

Restaurants overlooking the river, under the Torre del Infantado